Umrao Jan Ada

Mirza Muhammad Hadi Rusva

Translated by
David Matthews

RUPA

First published in 1996 by
Rupa Publications India Pvt. Ltd.
7/16, Ansari Road, Daryaganj
New Delhi 110002

Sales Centres:
Allahabad Bengaluru Chennai
Hyderabad Jaipur Kathmandu
Kolkata Mumbai

ISBN: 978-81-716-7311-7

Seventh impression 2019

10 9 8 7

Typeset by SÜRYA, New Delhi

Printed at Gopsons Papers Ltd, Noida

Contents

Translator's Preface

The novel, Umrao Jan Ada, which recounts the life-story of a courtesan of nineteenth century Lucknow, is one of the best-known and best-loved works of early Urdu fiction. Its authors, Mirza Muhammad Hadi Rusva, was born in Lucknow around the time of the 1857 'Indian Mutiny', which was a significant turning point not only in the life of the Princely States like Avadh (Oudh), but in the history of the country as a whole. After finishing his education, he was appointed as a teacher in the Central High School and then in the Christian College of Lucknow. He soon developed an interest in chemistry and other 'modern' sciences, such as psychology and logic, and gave up his teaching career in order to pursue them. Like many of his contemporaries he wrote Urdu poetry, and seems to have acquired a reasonable reputation for his verse, many lines of which embellish his novel. He also turned his attention to Urdu prose fiction, which in the time of his youth was something fairly new, and produced a number of short novels. Apart from Umrao Jan Ada, however, the rest of his work is now little read. It is interesting also to note that he is credited with the invention of an Urdu system of shorthand, which some would have us believe he used for writing down Umrao's dictated story. But whether Umrao Jan Ada actually existed or not is something we do not know. In his later years, Rusva moved to Hyderabad, where he worked for the translation bureau, known as the *Dar ut Tarjuma,* which was founded by the Nizam's government. He died there in 1931.

Like many of his fellow-citizens, Rusva had a high regard for the culture of Lucknow, which, as he remarks on a number of occasions in his novel, he felt had greatly declined in the years following the Mutiny. Indeed, his admiration for the customs and manners of Lucknow, and above all for the exquisite language of its inhabitants, is shared by many of his contemporary writers, whose works frequently idealize the era of the Nawabs, which they had not experienced, but of which, simply by being 'Lakhnavi' they felt they were a part.

The Sultanate of Avadh, of which Lucknow was the capital, was established in the first decades of the 18th century by rulers, calling themselves 'Nawabs', who originated from the Khorasan province of Iran. The first seat of government was in the town of Faizabad, some forty miles to the north of Lucknow. The Nawab, Shuja-ud Daula (1754-17775), careful not to waste too much of his money on grandiose architecture, constructed low temporary buildings, know as *bangla* (hence

English 'bungalow'). It was here that Umrao Jan Ada was born, and in her first encounter with the procuress, Khanam, she refers to her birthplace as *Bangla.* Shuja-ud Daula's successor, Asaf-ud Daula, moved the capital to a site on the river Gomti, which according to some was known as *Lakshman Tila,* 'The Mound of Lakshman', the younger brother of Lord Rama. In time, it is said, the Sanskrit name *Lakshman* developed into *Lakhnau,* spelt in English as Lucknow.

Being of Persian origin, the rulers of the Avadh Sultanate were Shi'as, those Muslims, who having espoused the cause of the Prophet's kinsman, Ali, and his son, Husain, broke away from the orthodox Sunni caliphs, and followed their own leaders, the Imams. One of the most prominent edifices in Lucknow is the great Imambara, 'House of the Imams', built during the reign of Asaf-ud Daula, where every year during the month of Muharram (the first of the Muslim calendar) Shi'as gather to mourn the death of Imam Husain, who was martyred at the battle of Karbala in 679 A.D.

The province of Avadh and its capital soon became extremely rich, and after Nadir Shah's devastating attack on Delhi in 1739, many noble families of that once splendid city moved eastwards to seek their fortunes there. In their wake followed some of Delhi's most distinguished poets, who in search of patronage brought with them their own language and culture. Until the fall of Avadh in 1857, Lucknow remained the undisputed cultural centre of the Urdu-speaking world, renowned not only for its 'sweet' language and verse but also for its music and dance, in which the courtesans, known as *tavaifs,* played an important part.

These courtesans were no ordinary prostitutes, and their best were highly skilled practitioners of the arts, who could command vast sums for their performances and other favours. As Umrao

Jan notes in the concluding pages of her account, courtesans often caused the ruin of some of the most illustrious noble families of the city. Even now many descendants of such families, who still cling to the title 'Nawab', will recall with some nostalgic fondness how their forbears were impoverished through their extravagance and profligacy.

The courtesan began her training in her childhood with a thorough grounding in classical Persian and Arabic, reading the standard works under the tutelage of a maulvi. The books mentioned in the novel, such as the *Gulistan* and *Bustan* of the 13th century Persian poet, Saadi, remained on the traditional school syllabus well into the 20th century, and many people still alive in India and Pakistan would have been brought up on them.

Maulvis, technically men who have studied the Quran and are qualified to impart religious instruction, were far from being dry clerics, and were very much part of the fabric of society. They usually married, and, as we can see from the novel, even formed liaisons with courtesans without incurring the opprobrium of their followers and fellow-citizens. In Urdu literature of all periods the maulvi with his kindly face, long white beard and fastidious habits has been the butt of good-natured satire. Rusva, however, not uncharacteristically adopting a high moral tone, can on occasions be quite scathing when he finds these 'pillars of the faith' exceeding the bounds of decency or showing themselves to be downright ignorant.

Besides Indian classical music and dance, the courtesan would also be encouraged to develop a taste for Persian and Urdu poetry. Umrao Jan Ada not only learnt the verses of the acknowledged masters by heart, she also composed poetry herself, for which connoisseurs held high regard.

Among Urdu-speaking people, poetry has been and still is

one of the most popular forms of entertainment. The *mushaira,* or 'poetic-gathering', to which poets are invited to recite their compositions, can still attract large audiences who never seem to tire of what they receive in sessions which can last for several hours at a time. The grandest *mushairas*, organized in the royal courts or palaces of nobles, would be splendid affairs governed by age-old conventions and rules of etiquette. Often the invitation would contain one line of a verse, known as a *tarah,* in the metre and rhyme-scheme of which the poet would compose his own offering. The most popular form of verse was the *ghazal,* a lyric with the rhyme scheme AA BA CA, etc. The last verse would contain the poet's nom-de-plume, which would usually be a noun or an adjective. The pen-name of the author of this novel was *Rusva,* which means 'Disgraced', that of Umrao Jan was *Ada,* meaning 'Coquetry'. The *ghazal* is usually associated with the expression of unrequited love, and its well-known imagery of the tulip and the rose, the flask of wine and the nightingale, the flowing black locks of the heartless beloved, the tears of blood shed by the forlorn lover, goes back to medieval Persia, where the lyric was first developed. The *ghazal* may, however, be devoted to many other subjects and themes, and its success depends upon the inventiveness and artistry of the poet. In the *mushaira*, which would be ordered by a master of ceremonies, a candle would be placed before the poet next due to recite. Etiquette often demanded that the poet would first make his excuses, saying that he had nothing fresh to offer. Coaxing from the other participants would reveal a poem of several choice verses concealed in his pocket! Usually the junior and comic poets would precede the great masters, who would take pride of place towards the end of the proceedings. In Lucknow especially, light relief might be provided by those who wrote their verse in a language and style usually associated with the speech of purdah ladies. Throughout the gathering the audience participated, and good verses would be greeted with shouts of "vah! vah!", "by the grace of Allah, indeed thou hast broken the pen!;" poor verses would come in for vociferous criticism and booing.

Mushairas could also be informal, spontaneous events when a few friends might gather in the intimacy of their own home, and a good example of this kind of private gathering is given in the opening pages of this novel. The role that poetry played in the society of the time makes the inclusion of verses in the narrative of the novel quite natural.

Poetic gatherings are by no means a thing of the past, and they still form an essential part of the social life of the Urdu-speaking population of India and Pakistan, where many people from all walks of life carry around their note-book of verses with them to be read out whenever the occasion arises.

Verse also played an important part in the major religious events of the year. During the first ten days of Muharram, when Husain's army was defeated at Karbala, Shi'as in particular organize meetings, known as *majlises,* in order to mourn the death of their Imam. The *majlis* is first addressed by an orator, who will recount the story of the battle. Then poets recite lengthy elegies before their committed audience of people who respond by weeping, beating their breasts and calling the words *'Ya Husain'! 'Ya Husain'!* On the tenth day, when the martyrdom occurred, people go around the streets in procession carrying replicas of Husain's tomb, known as *taziyas.* In Lucknow, a city with a high proportion of Shi'a Muslims, the Muharram mourning rituals, which include self-flagellation and walking barefoot over live embers, were particularly renowned, and it was in Lucknow that the Urdu elegy reached its height as a unique literary form. The greatest exponents of the *elegy,* or *marsiya,* were the 19th century poets, Mir Babar Ali Anis and Mirza Dabir ('Mir and Mirza'), whose works in this sphere are unrivalled. Expressions of grief were also set to music in the form known as *soz* (literally 'burning passion'), in which Umrao herself excelled. The introduction of music into religious ritual is frowned upon by orthodox Muslims, and it is probably for this reason that the art, which was cultivated in Lucknow, has declined.

While the Urdu poetic tradition goes back to the middle of the 16th century, and was firmly established by the middle of the 18th, prose developed much later, and for a long time the use of Persian as the most favoured prose medium persisted. After the events of 1857 and the subsequent establishment of British rule in India, many writers felt a growing need to communicate their feelings and responses in Urdu, which by this time had become one of the most highly developed languages of the subcontinent. Modern prose writing, both fiction and non-fiction, composed to a large extent under the influence of English, begins from this period. The first novels tended to be written with a view to instruction, and concentrated on social issues such as the evils of purdah, the education of women, the role of the Muslim in the modern world and so on. Many purely fictional works, however, still dealt with glorious past or recounted the traditional romantic tales.

Umrao Jan Ada, not least because of the daringness of its subject, is quite unusual for its time, and even now is greeted with mixed feelings by those who feel that such a frank description of a prostitute's life is not quite fit for members of a respectable society. Mirza Muhammad Hadi was no doubt proud of his ability to be broadminded, and obviously delighted in his pen-name, Rusva, 'The Disgraced.'

Compared to many other Urdu novels of the period, *Umrao Jan Ada* is fresh and vivacious; its plot is uncontrived and its language remarkably lucid and natural.

Little in the novel requires commentary or explanation. A few notes, marked * in the text, mostly dealing with minor historical and cultural points have been added in the appendix.

David Matthews
London 1994

Umrao Jan Ada

ہم کو بھی کیا کیا مزے کی داستانیں یاد تھیں
لیکن اب تمہیدِ ذکرِ دردِ ماتم ہوگئیں

How many tales of pleasure we recall—
A preface to the pain of sorrow's call.

My dear readers! The beginning of the story goes back about ten years, when a friend of mine, Munshi Ahmad Husain, a native of the Delhi region, paid a short social visit to Lucknow. He had rented a room in the Chowk* near the Sayyid Husain Gate, where during the evenings he would sit with his friends enjoying excellent conversation. Munshi Sahib had a fine taste in matters of poetry. He even managed to recite himself, and his compositions were good; but he much preferred listening to others. For this reason, verse and poetry formed the main part of our conversations. The room next to his was occupied by a courtesan. Her life-style was quite different from that of the other 'ladies of easy virtue'. No one ever saw her sitting on the balcony overlooking the street, nor was anyone ever heard entering or leaving her room. Day and night the curtains were drawn over the doors, and the entrance from the Chowk always remained tightly shut. Another doorway led into a narrow lane, and this was used by her servants. On occasions when the sound of singing came from her room, it was impossible to ascertain whether anyone else was present there or not. In the room where we held our gatherings there was a small window on the adjoining wall, but this was always covered by a cloth.

One day, our friends had gathered as usual, and someone was reciting his *ghazal.* The customary praise was given, and I recited one of my own verses. Suddenly from the direction of the window we heard the cry: *'vah, vah'!* I stopped and my friends turned to the window. Munshi Ahmad Husain called out: "Absent praise is not fitting. If you enjoy the verse so much, then come and join our company." There was no answer and I resumed my recitation. The whole matter was forgotten. After a short while, a servant-girl arrived and, greeting the whole assembly with a touch of her forehead, said: "Which one of you is Mirza Rusva?" My companions pointed to me.

The servant said: 'My mistress has summoned you.'

'Who is your mistress?,' I asked.

The servant answered: 'My mistress asked me not to disclose her name. Please do as you think fit.'

When I hesitated to follow the girl, my friends joked with me: 'Well, sir! What are you waiting for? You never know how safe you will be accepting such invitations!'

I was still wondering who this woman could be who had issued such an informal summons, when the maid said: 'Sir, my mistress knows you well, and for that reason has asked you to come along.'

I had no alternative but to go, and when I entered the room, all was instantly revealed. Sitting before me was no other than Umrao Jan Ada. She looked at me and began the conversation which proceeded as follows:

'By Allah, Mirza Sahib! You have forgotten me.'

'Who on earth could have guessed where you had disappeared to?'

'Well, I've often heard your voice, but I could never summon up enough courage to call you. But the *ghazal* you have just recited disturbed me. I couldn't help myself shouting out in praise. I heard someone calling me to join you, but modesty forbade me. I thought it better to keep silent, but finally I was unable to restrain myself. For past favours I troubled you, and humbly beg your pardon. Please recite that verse once more.'

'I shall neither pardon you, nor shall I recite my verse. If you really desire it, then you will have to join us.'

'I have no objection to coming, but I fancy that your host may be offended.'

'Really! How can you think such a thing? If that were the case, would I have invited you? It is an informal gathering. Your presence will give us even greater pleasure.'

'True. But I hope that there will not be too much informality.'

'Certainly not. When you are there, the only informality will be from me.'

'Very well, I shall come tomorrow.'

'Why not now?'

'No, no! Do you not see what a state I'm in?'

'But we do not expect a 'performance.' There is no formality at all. Please come.'

'Mirza, I have no answer to your persistence. You go along first, and I shall follow.'

I got up and left. After a short while, Umrao Jan Sahiba, having rearranged her hair and changing her clothes, joined us. I said a few words to my friends about her exquisite poetic taste and musical accomplishments, and all were eager to hear her. She listened to each of our compositions and then recited her own verse. In short, it was the most pleasurable gathering. And from that day onwards, Umrao Jan usually joined us for a couple of hours in the evening. Sometimes we recited our verse; sometimes she would sing for us. My friends were delighted, and here I shall do my best to describe the scene. In our sessions we had no pre-arranged pattern for metre or rhyme,* nor did we ask too many people. They were simple informal gatherings, where everyone would recite his own work.

The Mushaira

کس کو سنائیں حالِ دلِ زار اے اداؔ
آوارگی میں ہم نے زمانے کی سیر کی

Who will hear the sadness of my heart, Ada?
In wandering life's journey took us near and far.

'What a fine verse, Umrao Jan Sahiba,' I said, on hearing the couplet, which was the last of an earlier poem. 'But there must be others.'

'Praise, indeed Mirza Sahib,' she replied. But I swear that is all I can remember. I have no idea when I composed it. Memory fades, and I've lost the wretched manuscript.'

'What was the first verse? enquired Munshi Sahib. 'I never heard it.'

'Of course not,' I said. 'You were too busy making the arrangements.'

And there could be no doubt about the fact that Munshi Sahib had taken great pains over that evening's gathering. It was the hot season, and an hour or so before sunset, the balcony had been sprinkled with fragrant water, so that it should be cool in the evening. A spotless white cloth had been spread on the ground. Brand new pitchers filled with perfumed water were placed on the coping. Earthenware goblets stood upon them, and ice had been prepared separately. In each of the paper pots were placed seven betel leaves wrapped in gauze and perfumed with fragrance, and on the lids a little fragrant chewing tobacco was strewn. The hookah pipes had been garlanded. Since it was a moonlit night, there was no need for too much illumination. Only one chandelier had been lit for the purpose of the recitation. As the clock struck eight, all our friends including Mir Sahib, Agha Sahib, Khan Sahib, Shaikh Sahib and Pandit Sahib assembled. After all had been served a refreshing butter-milk drink, the poetry began.

Munshi Sahib requested me to conduct the proceedings, but I refused this onerous task. Umrao recited the first verse of the poem she had previously quoted from:

I left the temple and the Kaaba was my star;
My faith was saved; my Lord gave favours from afar.

'Bravo!' cheered Munshi Sahib.

'Indeed,' added Khan Sahib, 'it's a fine exordium, but rather masculine in tone.'

Umrao teased him: 'Why, Khan Sahib! Should I then have adopted the language of women?'*

'Perhaps there's something to be said for that. After all,

"My Lord gave favours" sounds good from your lips.'

I joined in the discussion: 'So, you've begun your onslaughts already, Khan Sahib. But let's hear the poem first. If we all provide our commentaries, we shall never be able to enjoy the verse. *Every lane in the town has a scent of its own.*

Khan Sahib frowned but at last gave in.

'So, Umrao,' I said, 'recite another poem for us.'

She thought for a while, trying to recall the words, and began with a single line:

This night of separation will not die. . . .

This met with approval from the whole company. She accepted the praise by touching her forehead. 'Thank you. Now listen to this verse:

The cries of lamentation fill the sky,
But heaven cannot fathom how or why.'

'Excellent,' I said, echoing the general sentiment.

'You are too kind,' said Umrao continuing:

The beggars of the street wherein you dwell
Pour scorn on riches, thinking them a lie.

'Good! Good! Proceed!'

Someone had to lose his soul for sure;
This life does not easily pass by.

'Have you marked the verse, Khan Sahib?' I said.

'Indeed I have,' he replied. 'By the grace of Allah! The words were well said.'

Umrao was touched. 'Thank you, gentlemen,' she said. 'You are really too kind. But for your generosity. I am nothing.

It's certain that my lover will not come,
But still I fix the portal with my eye.'

Khan Sahib and the Pandit were enraptured, and begged her to continue.

Though I have hope, at last I am resigned.
So why complain about my destiny?

Khan Sahib again commented: 'Another fine verse, but I detect a touch of Persian.'

'Be that as it may,' said Munshi Sahib. 'The theme is pleasing. Continue, Umrao.'

Ah, hunter! We, your prey ensnared by love,
Have no desire for wings to help us fly.
A misfired glance strayed from the goal it sought
And never reached my own poor heart. But why?

'Indeed, it should have done,' said Khan Sahib, inviting the final verse.

Ada, the heart alone knows of the heart;
Obedience is the path I shall not try.

'An excellent finish,' said Khan Sahib. 'You obviously

speak from your own experience, but this runs contrary to most people's opinion.'

'My own experience is another matter,' replied Umrao. 'The subject I chose is merely poetic.'

The company expressed various views, but all agreed on the pearl-like quality of her verse. Umrao stood up and took her bow, while Munshi Sahib urged Khan Sahib to recite something. Pleading that he could hardly remember anything, he began with the first verse:

The daughter of the vine eludes my sight:
In one whole month I do not have one night.

'Well done! That must be the night of the new moon,' I shouted. 'Continue.'

Praise for well-hewn verse I have received;
But every time desire is put to flight.

'That is excellent,' I shouted again. 'Another verse!'

My fickle love once gave me all I craved.
But now rejects my every plea outright.

At this point someone else entered, carrying a lantern. Khan Sahib addressed him: 'Who is that? What need is there of a lantern on a moonlit night?

'I do beg your pardon. That was stupid.'

'Good heavens, it's Nawab Sahib! Never mind. No harm done.'

The Nawab took his place. Everyone greeted him and asked him to recite a *ghazal*. He replied that he had only come to listen to us, and could remember nothing at that moment. Shaikhsahib, however, insisted, and the Nawab responded with the only verse he could call to mind:

The murderer's glance will find the heart one of these days;
The lethal shaft will play its part one of these days.

The whole company praised the verse. The Nawab accepted it, but after that remained silent, still insisting that he could remember nothing else. And so Pandit Sahib was asked to grace us with his composition. He obliged us:

We met but there was only mention of my rival's name;
For me the wine from her wild eyes and poison were the same.

Accepting our praise, the Pandit went on:

My pious friends! For two whole days now we have talked of God;
If not, then would the Kaaba echo with the idol's name?

'I can't say,' said the Nawab, but it's a good verse.'

'Whether you can say or not,' retorted the Pandit, 'it's still true. Listen to this:

The one who bends his neck to kiss the ground on which she treads,
To whom, oh wise adviser, would he bow his neck in shame?

We praised the verse and he continued:

In praise of her long locks how many scrolls have been unwound;
Oh men of faith! Your scattered wits were counted in her name.

'That is Lucknow wit,' I remarked.

'Since when have you come from Delhi?' joked the Pandit. 'I just thought I would mention it. Please continue.'

My heart was once a new-blown rose in the garden of my will;
But then the thorns of longing for love's pain and torment came.

The Nawab praised the verse, Khan Sahib noted the depth of expression, and the Pandit invited us to hear the last verse:

Makhmur! When did you thank Him for the grace He showed to you?
For every breath you took was given to you in God's name.

Khan Sahib was enthusiastic. He even quoted a Persian maxim: 'By the grace of Allah! Every breath is a unique pearl of the Holy Prophet, when it cometh as a delight of the Lord.'

'Khan Sahib,' I said, 'with you around, it is difficult to recite a poem without interruption.' The whole company joined in the praise. The Pandit very graciously accepted our kind words, and Munshi Sahib requested Shaikh Sahib to give us one of his compositions. Shaikh Sahib smiled and, feigning modesty, told us that he could remember nothing.

'You can't remember? retorted Khan Sahib. 'I bet you have a seventy-verse *ghazal* tucked away in your pocket.'

'I swear,' answered Shaikh Sahib, 'that I have only managed

to get four of the verses right.'

'Well, let's hear them then!' I said. Shaikh Sahib began:

A real request from all demand is free;
No denial in vows made honestly.

Shaikh Sahib acknowledged our appreciation:

Like Joseph you go round the market place;
No shame if there is none to pay the fee.

I thought that the Shaikh's verse showed taste, and bade him go on:

The heart shunned by the beauty's gaze is well:
Those goods no one can buy have quality.

Shaikh Sahib began the last verse of his poem:

Your oath to kill your lover proved untrue;
Until you take the sword, I won't agree.

At that moment, a gentleman entered and handed a note to Munshi Ahmad Husain. He read it and told us that Mirza Sahib would not be joining us. He had, however, sent along his latest composition. I asked the reason for his absence, and the gentleman told us that he had received a consignment of English saplings, which he was planting on the edge of the pool, known as Gol Hauz. The gardener was watering them.

'Never mind,' said Munshi Sahib. 'Read his poem. He really has spoilt our pleasure. Let's hear it.'

'Won't you ask me to recite something?' I asked.

'Of course,' said Munshi Sahib. 'We'll hear your *ghazal* first.' I began:

Do not ask me how my days of grief and pain pass by;
In separation from my love I neither live nor die.

Even now the plaintiff laughs as he waits for the noose;
When salt is rubbed into his wounds, how happily he'll cry.

I asked her for a kiss; do you rejoice if I'm deceived,
When she's deceived so many of her lovers with her sigh?

In separation someone takes her name and dies of grief;
Let those who fear disgrace pay heed; far better not to try.

Alas fate has destroyed me; there is no way I can mend.
Whoever saw dishevelled locks redressed and piled high?

At one time she reviled the comb; one time she broke the glass;
Composure quickly turned to anger; anger soon passed by.

Her sweet young breasts will be my death, their charms my sure demise;
See how they rise when as she walks her shawl becomes awry.

*Rusva means 'disgrace,' Ada means 'grace,' so who is chaste?**
Let no one ask why those who die for someone wish to die.

My friends applauded every verse, and now it was time to hear the poem that Mirza Sahib had sent:

Last night when somehow she came late to me,
The world grew dark; I lost the power to see.

My death approaches; now perhaps, Oh Life!
My very heart and soul grow tired of thee.

These stupid wishes would not let me live
If I gave in and let them conquer me.

Ah Death! What happened that thou dids't not come?
It took her just as long to come to me.

Of my destruction now thou hast the news.
Why dost thou ask me how my life might be?

Today I asked her: 'Swear that thou wilt come.'
I almost died when she came late to me.

My wish to sin was cowered like a cat;
By fondling it became a lion born free.

Today's mushaira is not graced by Mirza.
It's growing late. No need to wait for me.

After the poem was read out, a poet by the name of Mazhar-ul Haqq, who had come from some other town to join our gathering, recited this poem, in which he had some truth to tell about our modern-day *mushairas*:

Of our mushairas listen to a tale.
Your commentator's story will not fail.
Now people laugh at those who know the art,
And ridicule those adepts who take part,
What times we live in! What a situation!
Sweet poesy has lost its reputation.
Although men act politely to our face,
A little satire's not quite out of place.
The poets come along—a merry band—
And bring a crowd of friends to hold their hand.
They never come alone, they have a crowd
Of connoisseurs to call their praise aloud.
They have an army ready for the fray,
Like gladiators poised to thrust and slay.
But any poet lacking such a throng
Will never hear much cheering for his song.
From one side comes the shout 'Bravo! Bravo!'
The other echoes with 'Aha! Oho!'
'Ah! Thou hast scattered pearls before our session.'
'What words thou fashionest! And what expression!'
One cries: 'Ah! What he said!' with greatest tact.
(Another wonders what he's said, in fact).
'No one speaks more to the point or faster;
My God! He's even better than his master.'
'You are the greatest poet of our time.
*Compared to Mir and Mirza - more sublime!**
I can't recall such beauty in their verse,
Which was alright, but yours is far more terse.
They wrote quite well about the sword and fetter,
But, oh my God, your writing's so much better!
They weren't so good, they just acquired a name.
But nothing to compare with your great fame.

Those bards belong to ancient history.
Your style has subtler points, more mystery.
Before you no one dares a word to utter;
Just listen to their mumbling and mutter!
This gift you have was written in your fate;
You had this magic handed on a plate.
We've searched our hearts and come to the conclusion
That you are you, and you without collusion.
And we alone can tell just what you are;
You're as you are, and as you are you are.
But do you know your worth? Perhaps you don't.
We'll tell you what you're like but others wòn't.
*Was any other poet born like you?**
There never was and never will be. True.
In short, they lap the praise up they've received,
And never dream they might have been deceived.
Such praise is useless, though it's laid on thick.
It really is enough to make you sick!
But if they're criticised, they bawl and shout.
And often stop their critics with a clout.
You shouldn't be surprised at what you see.
It's even happened once or twice to me.
Their weighty words with gravity resound;
They touch their foreheads, bowing to the ground.
They seem to be so modest from afar.
But in their hearts they think, 'How great we are!'
They put on airs and graces, strut and prance;
And often praise themselves when they've a chance.
They give a commentary on every word
To make quite sure you've grasped the verse you've heard.
They love the praise we give them from the heart,
And know that we appreciate their art.

They keep their distance from the hoi polloi;
Standoffishness is their most favourite ploy.
These poets so discerning and sagacious,
Like those who praise are equally rapacious.
But what's the point of praise where it's not due?
Can you enjoy it when it is not true?
For these harsh words I know I'll get the blame,
But I'll stand by my theories just the same.
And my outspokenness will win the day.
I'll get what I deserve for what I say.
I'm fearless and that's not against the law;
I've told the truth and I shall not withdraw.
I don't like flattery and stupid pride;
I couldn't even do it if I tried.
I get fed up with poets nowadays,
Those jackanapes who always ask for praise.
If someone tells you he's a rising star
In verse, be sure to greet him from afar.

The members of our company praised the outspokenness and fair-mindedness of the description we had heard. I remarked: 'You have shown warm appreciation of every verse we have heard this evening; Umrao Jan was even in a state of ecstasy; as for my own feelings/—well, do not ask me!'

'Indeed,' said Munshi Sahib. 'Now, Agha Sahib. It's your turn.'

Agha began with his exordium:

Now bring along the kind of things
That really make the heart feel glad:
Some boiled peas, a bottle of
The real strong stuff that makes you mad.

'That's a fine start, Agha Sahib,' called out the company. Straightaway he embarked on the second verse:

Let me find a subject fit
For recitation, my dear lad!
This second verse rhymes with the first,
And you'll agree that's not too bad.

We certainly agreed that it was not too bad at all. Agha announced that his third verse was particularly addressed to the young Nawab, who was wearing a light almond-coloured shirt and a thin muslin over-garment, which was unbuttoned in the front. In his hand he held a delicate fan which he moved to and fro:

In the winter when you meet me,
I'll not fear the icy gale;
If your locks are on my shoulder,
blankets are of no avail.

Acknowledging our praise, Agha continued:

Tell the madman. Qais, to nourish
*Sadness with the joys he's seen.**
Let Laila's camel feed upon
His heart's sweet buds while they're still green.

'Glory be to Allah,' shouted the Pandit. 'See what sustenance was found in his starvation!' We all agreed with his interpretation and let Agha continue:

You'd better tell the lovers here
To stem their tears before we meet;
The road to your house will be closed
If we have flooding in the street..

The Shaikh liked the verse. I turned to Khan Sahib: 'Khan Sahib, you have become silent. Have you no objections to raise?'

'Indeed,' said Agha, 'silence does not befit such a connoisseur of fine poetry.'

'You may think my praise a sign of my inability to comprehend,' said Khan Sahib, haughtily. 'That is why I maintain my silence.'

Agha Sahib continued:

The one to whom I give my heart
Will be coquettish, and of course
Will have the graces of a camel
And the knavery of a horse.

'A very bold promise,' we remarked. 'Go on.'

I shall split my heart wide open.
If you leave me in the night;
I shall bind myself completely,
If you vanish from my sight.

'Good,' we said.

In the plainness of your beauty
There are qualities quite rare;

No blackness in your teeth or eyes,
No pretty comb to dress your hair. *

Umrao exclaimed: 'Really! Day and night she will be sitting there with her hair like a haystack.'

'Yes,' mused Agha. 'The first pleasure will be in her homeliness; the second is that she will save herself quite a lot of money on make-up. Listen:

If she comes to ask for money,
I shall give it quietly;
There will be no ranting, raving,
Mumbling, muttering. It's on me!

Umrao was amused and could not contain her laughter.

'Right,' said Agha, 'but my beloved is becoming debased. Here's something in praise of her fragility and the slenderness of her waist:

In the column of your slender
Waist, I'll put a cross-like sign;
But thickheads will not understand
The meaning of this slender line.

Khan Sahib looked puzzled: 'Perhaps I'm the kind of thickhead to whom you are alluding. But for God's sake, what's all this nonsense about crosses and slender lines?

'Don't worry,' said Agha, "I'll explain. When accountants leave a blank in their ledgers, they draw a cross. From the cross written here, we see that the waist is so slender that it has become invisible. The second point to bear in mind is that a cross is made up of two intersecting lines. From this it emerges that the beloved's waist is first cut and then joined together again. In other words, in spite of her waist being invisible, the upper and lower halves of her body are still joined together.'

'A rather *slender* line of thought!' we said. 'If anyone did not know that, your verse would be incomprehensible:'

Ah yes!' agreed Agha. But I'm not writing for just anybody. I'm sorry that my *ustad* is no longer alive.* If he were, appreciation of my verse would be assured. Anyway, I give you the last verse. I am so sorry that no one likes my poetry:

Enough, oh Cossack! Stop your spirit
Ushering in Destruction's Day;
There'll be such commotion
If the armies of your themes hold sway.

After asking him to recite this last verse again, the Nawab remarked upon the strange pen-name 'Cossack.'

Agha Sahib explained: 'Please don't imagine that I am putting on airs, but there are two main reasons for my choice. The first is that your humble servant's ancestors used to roam the deserts and steppe of China robbing and looting. The second is that my late *ustad* used to call himself Sariq, the Arabic word for 'robber,' which was in fact quite appropriate. (Here his face reddened, because he stole all his themes from the poets of the past and versified them himself.) All you have to do is glance at his works, and you'll probably find nothing new at all. When I grasped the reins of the steed of fair poesy in my own hands, thinking that the general area of robbing and stealing befitted my dignity, I took the pen-name 'Cossack.' There's also a kind of waggishness in this title, and I have always made it my business to snatch subjects from former masters and make them my own property.'

'Congratulations!' said the Nawab and with that the mushaira came to an end. We had a glass or two of iced *falsa,* an extremely refreshing fruit cordial, and our friends departed to their homes. Left alone at last, Munshi Sahib spread the cloth and invited Umrao and myself to stay for dinner. While we were eating, Munshi Sahib requested Umrao to recite the first verse of her *ghazal* again:

Who will hear the sadness of my heart, Ada?
In wandering, life's journey took us near and far.

'You have undoubtedly had an eventful life. While you were reciting, the thought occurred to me that you might give us the pleasure of hearing about it.'

I was equally enthusiastic, but Umrao was against the idea. Since his early youth, our Munshi Sahib had been inordinately fond of reading the old romances. In addition to the *Arabian Nights* and the *Tale of Amir Hamza,* he had cast his eye over all the volumes of the *Garden of Fancy.* There were very few novels that he had not read. But after spending a few days with us in Lucknow, and listening to the elegant speech of those who really know the language, his taste for the artificiality and pomposity found in the works of most novelists had declined. The verse that Umrao had recited gave birth to the idea I have already mentioned. In short, Munshi Sahib's enthusiasm and my own strong encouragement left Umrao with little choice.

Umrao's own style of speech was extremely refined, and this was only natural. First, she had been brought up in the company of well-read, high-class courtesans; then she had enjoyed the company of princes and sons of Nawabs, and had even gained access to the royal court. She had seen things with her eyes that most people never heard of.

When she was relating her story to us, I secretly took down everything, and when I had finished writing it up, I showed her the draft. At first she was very angry, but could do nothing much about it. Finally, she read it herself, here and there correcting some details.

I first got to know Umrao when she was connected with the Nawab, whose parties I also used to attend. I therefore have no doubts that all she told us was one hundred percent correct. But that is my own opinion. My readers are free to make up their own minds.

Mirza Muhammad Hadi Rusva

1

لطف ہے کونسی کہانی میں
آپ بیتی کہوں کہ جگ بیتی

What pleasure can there be in any tale?
The story of my life or of the world?

Listen, Mirza Rusva Sahib! Why do you keep bothering me with your questions? What pleasure can you possibly expect to find in the story of someone so unfortunate as me? The account of one so unlucky, so aimless; someone who lost her home and brought disgrace on her family; someone cursed by her nearest kin and damned in both this world and the next? When you hear it, I do not expect you to be glad.

Since you insist, hear it, but listen well.

There is no point in seeking respect by mentioning the names of my fore-bears, and to be truthful, I do not know them. All I know is that my house was in a district on the outskirts of the town of Faizabad. The house was brick-built, while around it the other dwellings were built of mud, little hovels or tiled structures. The people who lived there were ordinary folk. There were some water-carriers, barbers, washermen, litter-bearers and so on. In the area where we lived, there was only one house as tall as ours, and that belonged to a person named Dilavar Khan.

My father worked at the tomb of Bahu Begum.* I have no idea in what capacity or how much he earned. All I can remember is that people called him *Jamedar.** I spent my days looking after and playing with my little brother, and he was so fond of me that he would not leave me for a moment.

At evening, when my father came home from work, you cannot imagine our joy. I would throw my arms around his waist, and my brother, crying 'Daddy! Daddy!' would run and cling to his coat. My father, with a broad grin, would fondle us and stroke our backs, then he would lift my little brother up to his lap. I well remember that he never came empty-handed. Sometimes he would produce a couple of sugar-canes, sometimes sweet cakes, or a leaf-cup of sesame *laddu.* Then the time came to share them and what a pleasure it was for us to squabble over the things he had brought! My brother would snatch the sugar-cane; I would get my hands on the cup of sweets. At this moment, my mother would call out from the tiled kitchen that our supper was ready. No sooner had my father sat down than I would start my badgering: 'Really, Daddy! You haven't brought me the dolls. Just look at my feet and see how my sandals are broken. You have no idea! And my chain hasn't come back from the goldsmith's yet. It will soon be time for my little cousin's weening ceremony. What on earth shall I wear? I don't care, but I really must have a new set of clothes for Eid. A really new suit!'

As soon as my mother had finished cooking, she called me. I went and came back with the bread basket and a brass dish of curry. The cloth was spread, mother served the food, and we all set to with relish. After dinner, we all said our thanks to God, father performed his evening prayer, and then we went to sleep. Father would be up at the crack of dawn to say his prayers. At that moment, I jumped up and once more my requests would begin: 'Daddy! Please don't forget my dolls today. Make sure you buy them. And when you come this evening, bring lots of guavas and oranges and. . . '

Having completed his morning prayer, my father, still telling his beads, would go up to the roof. There he would let his pigeons out, feed them and fly a couple in the air. In the meantime my mother, having swept around, would prepare breakfast, because my father had to leave for work at sunrise. That finished, my mother would sit down to her sewing, while I would take my brother for a walk around the village or go to the tamarind tree that stood by our door. I sat my brother down, and joined in the games of the boys and girls who were all of my own age. What happy days they were! I didn't have a care in the world. I ate the very best of food, wore the finest clothes, and looked much better off than the other children. At that time I was still so innocent and wide-eyed.

Our house was the tallest in the area: all the others lived in small tiled or wooden cottages. In front of our house there were two entrance halls. Before the main hall there was a tiled structure and on both sides small rooms. In front of that there was a kitchen, and on the other side were the stairs leading to the roof, where two more small rooms had been built.

We had more kitchen utensils than we needed, and several white cloths for eating off. People would often come to borrow these things from us. We employed a carrier to bring our water, while the other women of the area had to go to the well and fetch it themselves. When my father went out of the house, dressed in his uniform, people used to bow to him and greet him. My mother had a sedan; our neighbours used to walk.

I was also better looking than the other girls, though I must admit that I have never been a beauty. Of course, I wasn't as bad looking then as I am now. I had a light lotus-like complexion, and my features were not too bad. My forehead was on the high side, but I had big eyes and the round, plump cheeks of childhood. My nose may not have been acquiline, but it was not squashed and round like a wheel. I also had a good figure for my age, though I have not managed to keep it. I have never really been among the slimmest of people. I would wear red silk pyjamas with narrow ankles, a twill waist-band, a *nainsukh* blouse and a shawl of brocade; on my wrists I had three pairs of silver bracelets, a chain around my neck and a gold ring in my nose. But the other girls only had silver rings. My ears had just recently been pierced, and so all I wore were blue threads. My gold earrings had been ordered.

My marriage had already been arranged with my aunt's son, my father's nephew, and the engagement had taken place when I was nine years old. My in-laws were now getting impatient for the wedding. My aunt had been married in Nawab-Ganj, and her husband owned some land. Their house was quite a bit grander than ours, and I had already visited them with my mother before my engagement. The building was rather different from ours. The house was mud-built, but very spacious; in front of the thatched porch were tied oxen and buffaloes. There was never any shortage of milk or grain. In the maize season, corn-cobs used to arrive by the basket-full, and sugar-cane would be there, heap upon heap. You could always eat as much as you liked.

I had already seen my 'bridegroom'—that is the boy I was about to marry and had even played with him. My father had almost collected the whole dowry, and now it was just a matter of a few rupees. The marriage had been arranged for Rajab, the seventh month of the Muslim year.

During the late evenings, when my mother and father would be discussing my wedding, I used to creep up to the door to listen to their conversation. And how happy I would be! My young man was much better looking than Karima's—that was the name of the cotton-carder's girl, who was the same age as me. He was a black as pitch, but my boy was very fair: Karima's fellow had a thick, black beard, but mine had not even got his moustaches yet; Karima's groom went around in a dirty loin-cloth and wore a peagreen cap; but you should have seen mine when he was dressed up for the Eid in his green chintz padded coat, his satin pyjamas, lace hat and velvet slippers. Karima's boy wore a cloth over his head and walked around barefoot.

In short, I was very happy at that time, and could conceive of nothing better in life. It seemed that everything I had ever dreamed of was about to come true.

I can think of nothing unpleasant that befell me in my parents' home. Perhaps only the one time when I lost my silver ring while playing blind-man buff. The wretched thing was only silver, hardly worth more than an anna. Of course I can say that now, but at that time how could I have known how much things cost? I cried so much for that ring that my eyes were swollen. All day long I kept out of my mother's sight, but at night time, when she saw my finger bare, and asked what had become of the ring, I had to confess. My mother smacked my face; I shrieked, burst into tears, and cried till I got the hiccups. It was not until my father came home to console me and rebuked my mother that I calmed down.

Undoubtedly my father was more fond of me than was my mother. He never once touched me with the cane, but my mother would beat me for the slightest misdemeanour. She liked my brother best, and I got many a good hiding because of him. Still, I loved him very much. Sometimes just to spite my mother I refused to pick him up in the afternoons, but as soon as she had turned her back, I would rush to embrace him and take him in my arms. Then when I saw her coming again. I would put him down, and he would start to cry. My mother automatically thought that I was to blame for the tears, and started to bawl at me.

That's how she would go on, but if I had the slightest finger-ache, she would panic, refuse food and drink, and could not sleep until she had ordered medicine or some lucky charm. For my dowry she took the jewelled chain off her own neck and handed it to my father: 'Here, have a little more silver added,' she said, 'and brighten up the few new ones we have had made.' She took out most of her metal pots and had them re-plated, even though my father urged her to think of her own future. 'Oh never mind about that,' replied my mother. Your sister is the wife of a landowner, and I want her to know that her brother has also made a contribution. I don't care even if she is your sister. The in-laws' home has always had a bad reputation. If I sent my daughter along empty-handed, people will start to talk.'

2

ابتدا آوارگی کی جوشِ وحشت کا سبب
ہم تو سمجھے ہیں مگر ناصح کو سمجھائیں گے کیا

I know full well the terror of the time I went astray;
But oh adviser! Could you understand a word I say?

I have often heard people passing comments about those they call 'prostitutes' or 'courtesans.' Most dismiss them out of hand, pointing out that in the place where they grew up they witnessed nothing but evil ways. They just followed the example of their mothers and sisters, who were in the same state. But daughters of respectable parents who leave their home and follow the path to ruin deserve nothing more than to die in shame and degradation.

I have already described my own background, and have nothing more to say except it was afterwards that I went astray. From this you may have the impression that I was mad for sex. You might think that my marriage was delayed, and I set my sights on some other man; when he left me, I passed on to another, but being unsuccessful with him, by degrees I made it my profession. That is very often the case, and I have seen and heard of many respectable women who have gone bad in this way. There are several reasons for this. One is that the girl attains puberty, but the parents do not arrange the marriage in time; another may be that their marriage does not work out well for them. Their parents may have thrown them at the first man who came along, without considering his age, his looks or his temperament. They cannot get on with their husband, and find themselves out on the street. They might have suffered the awful blow of being widowed when they were still young. Losing patience, they remarried or found themselves in bad company. But in my case, it was a cruel stroke of fortune that led me into this miserable jungle, where there was no path other than that which led to ruin.

That wretched Dilavar Khan, whose house was only a short distance from ours, associated with robbers and ruffians. He had been in a jail in Lucknow for years, and at the time I am talking of he had been released on somebody's recommendation. He bore a grudge against my father, who had been among those in the district asked to supply an account of his character when he had been arrested in Faizabad. My poor father! He was so open and sincere that when the Queen's officer placed the Quran in his hand and said: 'Well, Jamedar! Tell me the truth now. What sort of man is he?' my father gave a completely fair description. It was mainly on his evidence that Dilavar Khan was sent to jail, or so I've heard from my mother.

The miserable wretch harboured rancour in his breast, and when he was released he also started to breed pigeons like my father. One day, he got hold of one of our pigeons, and was asking eight annas for its return. My father said he would give no more than four, and went off to work. For some reason that morning I was out early, and saw Dilavar Khan standing under our tamarind tree. He called me over: 'Here, little girl. Your daddy's paid me the eight annnas for the pigeon. You can come and fetch it now.' I fell into his trap, and went inside the house, but there was no sign of the pigeon. He was alone. As soon as I was inside, he fastened the door-chain. I wanted to cry out, but he stuffed a rag into my mouth and bound my hands tightly with a cloth. He sat me down on the floor, and going over to the front door called out the name of Pir Bakhsh, who came into the room. They both picked me up, took me outside and dumped me into a bullock-cart. Soon the cart began to move off. I was so agitated that I could hardly breathe; I had no power to do anything; those cursed men had me completely in their power.

Dilavar Khan was sitting in the cart, holding me down under his knee. He had a knife in his hand, and glared at me with his raging, blood-shot eyes. Pir Bakhsh was driving the oxen, which seemed to be flying along the road. The wind was howling and every part of my body was shivering with the cold. I gasped and tears were streaming down my cheeks; I could not imagine the terrible plight I was in. My father would be coming home from work and searching for me. My mother would be beating her breast, and my little brother would still be playing. How could he know of his sister's misery? My parents, my brother, the entrance-hall to my house, the court-yard, the kitchen-everything flashed in front of my eyes. On one side were these thoughts; on the other the fear for my very life. Dilavar Khan kept brandishing his knife. I thought he might plunge it into my breast at any moment. I no longer had the rag in my mouth, but I was stifled by fear. As I suffered in this way, Dilavar Khan and Pir Bakhsh kept laughing, shouting obscene insults at my parents:

'You see, Pir Bakhsh. A son of a soldier having his revenge after twelve long years! And what'll he be like now? Squirming!'

'Yes, mate. No doubt about that. You make the proverb ring true. You must have been inside for twelve years.'

'Twelve years to the day. You don't know what I went through in Lucknow. He'll pay for it. This is only the beginning. I'll have his life.'

'What? You mean you'll kill him?'

'What do you think? If I don't, I'm no son of a Pathan.'

'That's right, mate. You always do what you say. But what will you do with her?'

'Kill her, and chuck her in the gutter somewhere. Then we'll go home after midnight.'

When I heard this, I was certain of my death. The tears dried up in my eyes. My heart stopped beating. I was petrified. But seeing me like this, the wretched thug had no mercy. He thumped me so hard in the chest that I began to sob again. I was on the point of fainting. Pir Bakhsh remonstrated:

'Kill her? But what about my money?'

'You'll have it, I swear!'

'But where will you get it from? I had something else in mind.'

'Look, we'll go home. If I can't get any. I'll sell the pigeon.'

'Sell the pigeon? You're out of your mind. Can I make a suggestion?'

'What?'

'Well, take her to Lucknow and sell her.'

Now that I was sure that I was going to die, I had stopped hearing their miserable conversation. It seemed as if people were talking in a dream. But these last words of Pir Bakhsh at least gave me a little hope, and I began to ask God's blessing for him. Now all depended on Dilavar Khan's answer. He thought for a moment and replied:

'All right. We'll see. Now get a move on.'

'Wait a moment,' said Pir Bakhsh. 'Can't we stop here for a while? There's a fire burning under that tree. I'll go and get a light for the hookah.'

He went off, but all the time he was gone I was afraid that the other one might finish me off. To be in fear of one's life is a terrible thing. Suddenly, I cried out and this earned me several blows on the face from Dilavar Khan.

'Shut up, you little bastard. I'll really take my knife to you this time. I'll show you.'

Pir Bakhsh was some way off: 'No, no, mate! Don't do that. God save us! Let me get a light first.'

After a while he returned, filled the hookah and handed it to Dilavar Khan, who took a puff and asked: 'How much do you think we might get for her? And where could we sell her? If we get caught, there'll be real trouble.'

'Just leave it up to me,' said Pir Bakhsh. "We'll sell her alright. What are you worried about? And who'll catch us? These things go on day and night in Lucknow. You know my brother-in-law?'

'Karim?'

'Yes. That's what he does for a living. He's caught no end of children and made money out of them in Lucknow.'

'Where is he these days?'

'Where? His in-laws live on the other side of the river Gomti. He'll be there.'

'Okay, but how much does he get for a child?'

'Depends on her looks. If you're lucky, you'll get up to a hundred and fifty for her.'

'Don't be fool. A hundred and fifty for looks like that? You wouldn't even get a hundred.'

'Alright. But what will you get if you kill her? Nothing.'

After that, Dilavar Khan whispered something to Pir Bakhsh that I could not make out. All I heard was the answer: 'I know that. You're just stupid!'

3

دے پھڑکنے کی اجازت صیّاد
شبِ اوّل ہے گرفتاری کی

Oh captor! Give me leave to flap my wings;
This is my very first day in your cage.

You have heard of the first day of my captivity. The helplessness of my situation! I shall never forget it till my dying day. It still amazes me that I survived at all. How insensitive I must have been to have gone on living. Dilavar Khan, you misreable wretch! I know you have received your deserts in this world, but does that offer me any consolation? If I could have your limbs hacked to pieces, I would have no remorse. I am certain that day and night in your grave you suffer the torments of hell, and on the Day of Judgement, God willing, you will receive even worse.

In my home, how must my parents have been feeling? They must have been besides themselves with grief.

That is enough for today, Mirza Sahib. I shall continue tomorrow. My soul is brimming over; all I want to do is cry out aloud. . .

What will you get out of listening to this story of how I went astray? Better to leave it here. For my own part, I think it would have been better if Dilavar Khan had killed me there and then. My good reputation would have been covered by a handful of dust; there would have been no stain on the honour of my household; we would have all been spared the degradation in the eyes of the world.

Yes. I saw my mother once again, but that was a long time ago; God only knows if she still is still alive or dead. I have heard that my brother has a son, who will be about fifteen now. I have a strong desire to see them all, and it is no great distance to travel. These days it costs no more than a rupee to get to Faizabad. But that is impossible. I can do nothing about it. In those days when there was no train, the journey to Faizabad took four days. But Dilavar Khan, afraid that my father might catch up with him, took the long route, and God knows where we travelled for eight whole days. I was stupid, and had no idea where Lucknow was. All I gathered from their conversation is that was where they were taking me. I had heard the name of the city at home, because my mother's father worked as a door-keeper in some palace. My people used to talk about him, and once he came to Faizabad, bringing lots of sweets and toys. I can still remember what he looked like.

The cart crossed the Gomti, and they set me down in the

home of Karim's in-laws—a little mud-built hovel. Karim's mother-in-law, who looked like some horrible corpse-washer, took me and shut me up in a room. We had arrived in Lucknow early in the morning, and it was midday before the door of the room opened. A young woman—Karim's wife—brought in three chapatties, a dish of lentils and a beaker of water, and setting them down before me, went out again. The food seemed delicious; I had not eaten anything cooked for eight days. After eating, I stretched out my legs and fell asleep on the floor. I had no idea how long I slept, because in that dark room there was no way of distinguishing night from day. Several times my eyes opened. Everywhere there was darkness and not a soul to be seen. I again covered my face with my shawl and fell asleep. This happened four or five times, and finally I could sleep no more. I sat up and Karim's mother-in-law, looking like a witch, came in mumbling something:

'Just look how she sleeps, my little one! Crying all night and making herself hoarse. Shake her and she won't wake up. Can't even hear her breathing. I thought a snake had sniffed her. Oh look, she's up now!'

I listened to her muttering in silence. Finally she asked me where the cup had gone. I picked it up and gave it to her. She went out. After a while, Karim's wife came in and opened the window. She took me outside and led me to a broken ruin. From there I was able to see the sky. Then she took me back into the dark room, and gave me some water, a plate of lentils and a piece of millet bread.

I spent two days like this. On the third, they brought in another girl, who was two years older than me. I have no idea where Karim had picked her up. The poor thing was crying her eyes out. Her arrival was a blessing for me, and when she finally dried her eyes, we began to talk.

She was the daughter of a Hindu banya, called Ram Piyari, who lived in village near Sitapur. In the darkness I could not make out her features, but the next day, when as usual the window was opened, we had a good look at each other. She had a pretty face with a fair complexion; her body was on the thin side. They took her away on the fourth day, and once more I was left alone. On the third day after that, Dilavar Khan and Pir Bakhsh came at night to fetch me. There was a full moon. First we crossed a field, then a bazaar; after that we came to a bridge underneath which the river was gushing. I shivered in the cold wind. Then came another bazaar from which we entered a narrow lane. It was a long walk and my feet were getting tired. The lane emerged into another bazaar, which was thronged with people. Here we stopped at the door of a house.

Mirza Rusva, have you guessed which bazaar that was, where my virtue was sold? Of course, it was the Chowk. And that house, in which I received disgrace and honour, both ill and good repute, shame and glory, or whatever else exists in this world—yes, it was the house of Khanum Jan, where the door stood open to greet me. We ascended the stairs and went to the upper floor.

Crossing the courtyard into the main hall, we went to the right into another large portico, and I found myself in the presence of Khanum Jan. You must have seen Khanum. At that time she was about fifty, but what a grand old lady! Her complexion was rather dark, but I think I have never seen a woman so elegantly dressed. The ringlets in the front of her hair were white, and suited her face. She wore a white muslin head-scarf of impeccable taste, and purple pyjamas which were very wide at the ankles. The thick, solid gold bangles on her wrists and the plain ornaments attached to her ears added to her splendour. Her daughter, Bismillah, resembled her exactly in her face and complexion, but lacked the charm of her mother. To this day I can remember just how Khanum looked, sitting on the floor with her back resting on a low couch.

A chandelier illuminated the room. In front of her, a large ornamental pan-box* was lying open. She was smoking a hookah. A darkish girl, who turned out to be Bismillah, was dancing before her, but on our arrival, the dancing stopped and the other people left the room. All had been arranged beforehand.

'Is this the girl?' Khanum Jan asked Dilavar Khan.

He nodded and she summoned me before her. She patted my head and tilted my forehead up in order to get a good look at my face. 'Very well,' she said. 'It is as we arranged, but where is the other girl?'

'That's already been settled,' said Pir Bakhsh.

'How much for?'

'Two hundred.'

'Really? Where?'

'A lady bought her for her son.'

'She had a nice face. I would have given you the same. But you were hasty.'

'What can I do about it? I told this bloody fellow. He wouldn't listen.'

Dilavar Khan broke in: 'Her face is all right as well. Do what you like.'

'Well, she's somebody's child.'

'That's all I've got for you anyway.'

'If you insist,' said Khanum, calling out the name of Husaini.

Husaini, a plumpish, dark-skinned middle-aged women

appeared. Khanum ordered her to bring the chest and handed Dilavar Khan a great bundle of rupees. Later I learned that she had paid one hundred and fifty for me. Of this sum, Pir Bakhsh was given fifty, which he wrapped up in his face-cloth. Dilavar Khan stuffed the rest into his pocket. Both politely bowed before Khanum and left. Khanum, Husaini and I were now alone in the room.

'Well,' said Khanum to Husaini. 'I don't think we paid too much for her.'

'No, I would say that we got her cheap.'

'Not exactly cheap, but even so. She's got an innocent face. God knows who she belongs to. How terribly her parents must be suffering. Where did they get her from? Do those ruffians have no fear of God? But, my dear Husaini, we are quite innocent. It is they who will pay for their sins. If we hadn't taken her, she would have been sold elsewhere.'

'She'll be all right with us, Khanum Sahib. Haven't you heard how some ladies treat their maids?'

'Of course I have. Why, not so long ago I heard how Sultan Jahan Begum branded her girl with a red-hot skewer when she caught her talking to her husband.'

'True, you can do what you like in this world, but such ladies will have their faces blackened on Judgement Day.'

'Faces blackened? They'll suffer the fires of hell!'

'Quite right too. It's no more than such wretched people deserve.'

After that, Bua Husaini addressed Khanum, almost pleading with her: 'Ma'am, please let me look after this girl. She's your property, but I'll serve you well.'

Khanum agreed.

All this time, Bua Husaini had been standing. Now she sat down beside me and began this conversation, through most of which I was in tears:

'Well, little girl, where do you come from?'

'Bangla.'

'And where's Bangla?'

Khanum interrupted to point out that Bangla was another name for Faizabad.*

'And what's your daddy's name?'

'Jamedat.'

Khanum again interrupted: 'Really, Husaini, how could she know her father's name? She's only a child.'

'And what's your name?'

'Amiran.'

Once more Khanum chimed in: 'That name won't do at all. Let's call her Umrao.'

'Did you hear that, child? said Husaini. 'You must now answer to the name of Umrao. And when the mistress calls 'Umrao,' you must answer 'Yes, ma'am.'

From that day onwards my name became Umrao. Later when I joined the company of the prostitutes, people started to call me Umrao Jan.*

To her dying day, Khanum addressed me as Umrao, but Bua Husaini out of respect called me Umrao Sahib. When all this had been decided, Bua Husaini took me to her room, fed me, gave me sweets, made me wash my hands and face, and put me to sleep by her side.

That night, I dreamt of my parents, and saw my father coming home from work with the cup of sweets in his hands. My little brother was playing in front of him as he shared out the sticks of candy. He asked if I was in the portico, and if mother was in the kitchen. Then seeing my father, I rushed towards him, embraced him and told him all that had happened to me.

I must have cried and screamed so much in my sleep that Bua Husaini woke me up. When my eyes opened, the house and the portico had disappeared; my mother and father had vanished. I was crying in Bua Husaini's lap, and she was wiping my tears. In the light of the lamp, I saw that she also had tears in her eyes.

Bua Husaini was really a very kind-hearted lady. She was so good to me that within a few days I completely forgot my home. And why not? First, I had no alternative, and, as they say, you have to change your ways according to circumstances. I was given the best of food—dishes I had never tasted before—and was handed clothes to wear that I had never even dreamt of. I had three companions to play with—Bismillah Jan, Khurshid Jan and Amir Jan. Then there was dancing and singing day and night, parties, fairs, excursions to the gardens. In short, no luxury was spared.

Mirza Sahib, you must be thinking that I was hard-hearted to forget my home so quickly and join so readily in the games. Although I was very young, as soon as I joined Khanum's household, I realised that I was there for the rest of my life. Just as a new bride on her arrival at the house of her in-laws understands that she has not come as a guest for a couple of days, but will be there to live and die. I had suffered such pain at the hands of those cursed robbers that for me Khanum's house was like paradise. I knew that it was impossible to go back to my parents, and there was no point in hoping for what I could not have. Although Faizabad is only about eighty miles from Lucknow, it seemed an enormous distance to me. What a difference there is in the way adults and children think about things.

4

اک حال میں انساں کی بسر ہو نہیں سکتی
اب رنگ طبیعت کا بدل جائے تو اچھا

A man can never stay in one fixed state;
And if his style and manners change, it's well.

I think Mirza, that you remember Khanum's house. You know how huge it was and how many rooms there were. All of Khanum's 'girls' resided there. Khanum's daughter, Bismillah, and Khurshid were the same age as I was, but we were not yet classed as fully-fledged 'prostitutes.' Apart from us, there were a dozen or so girls who had separate rooms and their own staff. They presided over their own 'courts,' each one more beautiful than the other. They were all decked with jewels, and what elegant dresses they wore! But the kind of plain clothes we had for everyday wear other prostitutes never even had on festive days. Khanum's house was like a fairy-land. Every room you entered echoed to the sound of laughter and merriment, singing and music. I might have been young, but women are very clever and know exactly what they want. When I saw Bismillah dancing, I also had a longing in my heart to do the same. Without realizing it, I began to hum and imitate their postures by myself, and it was at that time that my 'education' began. I was naturally gifted in music, and was developing quite a fine voice.

After I had mastered the scales, my *ustad* began with fragments of melody. He taught extremely methodically, and every note of the raga had to be learned by heart and produced exactly by the voice. You could never get away with flattening a sharp, or going slightly off pitch. And I had the habit of asking questions. At first the *ustad* (may he be spared his shame in the grave!) would hedge.

One day I was singing the raga *Ram Kali* before Khanum. I sang the sixth note of the scale, known as *dhaivat,* sharp, but the teacher did not correct me. Khanum asked me to repeat. I did the same thing, but the teacher still did not correct me. Khanum peered at me, and I looked at the teacher, who hung his head in shame. Then Khanum really went for him:

'Ustad Ji! What was that?' *Ram Kali* requires the *dhaivat* note, and that was not correct. Once again, I ask you. Should the note be sharp or flat?'

'Sharp.'

'Then why did you not correct her?'

'I didn't notice it.'

'Didn't notice it? That's why I asked her to repeat. Even then you sat tongue-tied. Is that the way to teach young ladies?

If she were to sing like that in front of connoisseurs, they would spit on me.'

The teacher, firmly put in his place, remained silent, but thoughtful. He considered himself an expert, and that day greatly resented Khanum's interference.

One day, I happened to be singing *Soha.* Khanum was also present, and I asked the teacher if the *gandhara* mode should be half-flat or flat.

'Flat,' he replied.

'Khan Sahib!' exclaimed Khanum. 'Really, how can you say such a thing in my presence?'

'Why? Is there something wrong?'

You ask me what is wrong. Is *gandhara* ever flat in this raga? Tell me, please.'

'Yes, yes. Half flat?'

'So you agree. Are you trying to mislead the girl, or test me? You know, Khan Sahib, that I'm no expert. But in all humilty I can say that there is little that my ears have not heard. I was not trained in any old house. You must know of Miyan Ghulam Rasul. But what's the use? If you wish to teach, then do it with sincerity, If not, then I'm sorry. I shall make other arrangements. Please don't ruin my girls.'

'Very well!'

With these words, the *ustad* got up and for a few days we did not see him. Khanum took over the lessons herself. Finally, Khalifa Ji intervened, and after a great deal of mutual asseveration, both parties were united. From that day, the *ustad* taught very accurately, since he really had no alternative. He had underestimated Khanum. Through the whole of my life I have wondered whether Khanum knew more than the *ustad* or *vice versa,* because there were so many things that Khanum could explain, of which the *ustad* had no knowledge. Or it might have been the case that he failed to explain on purpose. These people can often swear to high heaven that they are honest, but are reluctant to part with their secrets. I became so interested that if ever I was unclear, or thought that the teacher was tricking me, I would go to Khanum. She was delighted with my enthusiasm, and would curse Bismillah. She had taken so much trouble over the girl, but apart from simple tunes and folk-songs she could produce nothing. She would even get the melody wrong.

Khurshid did not have a good voice. She had a face like a fairy, but a throat like split bamboo. She was excellent at dancing, which she had learned perfectly. Her performance only consisted of dance, but she would sometimes attempt a simple song, just to show that she could rise to the occasion.

Among Khanum's 'seniors' was a girl called Bega Jan, who was unsurpassed in singing. But if you saw her face even on a dark night you would run away in fright. She was as black as the bottom of a frying-pan, and you could press half a pound of mincemeat into her pock-marks. She had blood-shot eyes, a flat nose, squashed up in the middle, thick lips, large teeth, and was so fat that people named her 'the dwarf-elephant.' But her voice was exquisite and her knowledge was also very good. You just had to hear the modulation of her vocal chords to appreciate it. I would often go to her and badger her with my requests:

'Bega Jan! Just go over the scale with me.'

'Listen then: *sa, ri, ga, ma, pa, dha, ni.*'

'No, that's not what I want. Do the notes separately for me.'

'Oh, my girl! You get on my nerves. Why don't you go and ask your teacher?'

'No, Baji. You tell me. Please.'

'Oh, very well! sa (4) *re* (3) *ga* (2) *ma* (4) *pa, dha* (3) *ni* (2).

Twenty-two. Got it?'

I would be a bit naughty. 'No, I forgot to count them. Show me again.'

'Go away. I'll tell you nothing.'

'I'll get it out of you.'

'Listen, I've already told you. Don't bother me again.'

'All right. Last time. Let's count again. Two in *'ni'*, right?'

'Yes, two.'

'Good. There are twenty-two. Now run through all the scales.'

'Be on your way! Come tomorrow.'

'Look, I'll fetch the *tanpura.* Sing something for me.'

'What, for example?'

'Dhanasari.'

'What shall I sing. *Astai ? Dhrupad ? Taranna ?'*

'Wonderful! Sing a *dhrupad.'*

'Listen then:

'When my lover comes to me,
My body's fire from me will part.
Let me see my lover once,
And I shall write him in my heart.
I wait the whole night long for him;
When will he come? When will we meet?
The one who sees my lover first,
I'll lay my head upon his feet.

In Khanum's house, the girls learnt not only how to dance and sing, but also how to read and write. For this purpose she had set up a school, and there she employed a maulvi.* I was sent to the school in the usual way. I can still picture the maulvi, his bright, holy face, his white clipped beard, his clothes fashioned like those of mystics. On his fingers he had fine rings, set with turquoise and cornelian; he carried a rosary made from the soil of Karbala,* a board on which to rest his head while praying, and a stick which had a pure silver knob. Along with his other paraphernalia he had a small hookah, and a little pot of opium. What impeccable taste! He was also a man of principle and old-fashioned manners. At one time he happened to have had a liaison with Bua Husaini, which he still maintained. Bua Husaini also regarded him as her 'husband' in both the spiritual and worldly sense. Hearing the conversations which took place between these two elderly people, you had to admit that the younger generation could not compete with them.

The maulvi had a home somewhere in Zaidpur. He had been blessed with a house, a wife and several young sons and daughters, but since he had come to Lucknow to pursue his studies, he had probably not been back there more than half a dozen times. More often than not, his relatives would come to meet him in Lucknow. He would occasionally receive something from home, and Khanam paid him a salary of ten rupees. This went to Bua Husaini, who looked after his food and drink, hookah and opium expenses. In other words, she was his 'cash-keeper.' She also had his clothes made from him. Khanum greatly respected the maulvi, and it was really because of him that she had so much regard for Bua Husaini.

As you know, Bua Husaini had taken the responsibility for bringing me up, and for that reason, the maulvi was particularly attentive to me. I cannot tell you myself how highly he thought of me, for that would be against the rules of modesty and politeness. He gave me more encouragement that he did the other girls, and made an unhewn block like me into a human being. It is due to the beatings I suffered from his slippers that

I have been honoured above my station in all the aristocratic or noble houses I have entered. Because of this I have had the courage to open my mouth in the gatherings of such learned connoisseurs as yourself. I pride myself on taking part in the functions of the royal courts and in my attendance at the assemblies of ladies from the highest classes.

The maulvi taught me with great kindness. When we had finished the alphabet, we were introduced to the basic Persian language texts, such as the *Karima* and the *Mahmudnama.* Having learnt the *Ahmadnama* off by heart, we embarked upon Shaikh Saadi's *Gulistan.* The maulvi would teach two sentences and make us commit them to memory. We were taught the meaning of each word, especially in the verses, and could repeat the constructions. Emphasis was put on reading and writing; our spelling was checked; and we were given letters to write. After mastering the *Gulistan,* other Persian texts were easy to me. It seemed that we had already done the lessons. We then studied Arabic grammar and a few books on logic. I sat at the maulvi's feet for about eight years. You know yourself how fascinated I was by poetry, and have no need to go into the details now.

5

ہم نہیں ان میں جو پڑھ لیتے ہیں توتے کی طرح
مکتبِ عشق و وفا تجربہ آموز بھی تھا

We are not those who like the parrot utter what we hear;
The school of love and faith gave us experience in life.

In the school there were three girls including me, and one boy whose name was Gauhar Mirza. He was extremely naughty and badly behaved, and teased all the girls. He would make faces at one, he would pinch another and pull another's plaits or box her ears. Once he tied two girls' pigtails together. Sometimes he would break a pen-nib and sometimes deliberately turn an ink-pot over on a book. In short, we were all thoroughly fed up with him. In turn, the girls would thump him, and the maulvi would prescribe the punishment he deserved, but his pranks never ceased. I was his favourite target because I was the simplest and most naïve in the class, and was always the maulvi's pet. I would repeatedly tell the maulvi about him, and got him no end of beatings, but the shameless boy would not give in. Finally even I became tired of telling tales. When the maulvi heard my complaints, he thrashed him so mercilessly that I started to feel sorry for him.

In fact it was Bua Husaini who was responsible for the boy's arrival at our school.

Nawab Sultan Ali Khan was a noble from a very high ranking family. He lived in the Top Darvaza, and had a liaison with the *domni,* Banno.* Gauhar Mirza was her son. Although the Nawab had long since stopped seeing Banno, he still paid her ten rupees a month for the boy's upbringing, and sometimes behind the Begum Sahiba's back would meet her secretly. Banno lived in Qazi Bagh, where Bua Husaini's brother had his house. Gauhar Mirza had been a little terror from his early childhood, and the whole neighbourhood was thoroughly fed up with him. He would throw clods of earth through peoples' windows, and once asked a boy if he could see his bird-cage. The boy let him have it, whereupon he opened the wire door of the cage and all the birds flew away. There were many such incidents. Finally in desperation, his mother sent him to study with a maulvi in the local mosque, but even there he did not improve and began to disturb all the other boys. Once he put a frog down one of their shirts, then he tore one of their hats, and then threw one of their slippers into a well. One day the maulvi was saying his prayers, and Gauhar Mirza floated the maulvi's new high-heeled slippers on the pond. He then sat back to see what would happen. But the maulvi caught him, and smacked his face till he grew red. He then dragged him back home to his mother. When he reached Banno's house, he called out: "I refuse to teach your boy any more." And with that he stormed off. Gauhar Mirza, with a long face and tears in his eyes, went into the house where at that moment Bua Husaini happened to be chatting with Banno. Seeing the boy's plight, she took pity on him, and not being aware of his previous misdemeanours, cursed the maulvi:

"That maulvi's worse than a butcher. Look at the poor boy's face. It's all swollen from the beating. There's even blood trickling from his ear. You can't let him be taught like that. Our maulvi's a good, kind man."

Without a moment's hesitation Banno said: 'Please, Husaini. Please take him to your man.

'I'll certainly take him, but it's a very long way for him to go.'

'Never mind. I'll send him with your brother in the morning and bring him back myself in the evening.'

The matter was agreed between them. Bua Husaini had no need to ask our maulvi, and she was absolutely confident that he would not refuse.

The next day, Ali Bakhsh, Bua Husaini's brother, balancing a large tray of sweets on his head, arrived with the boy. Buva Husaini merrily distributed sweets and introduced him to the maulvi.

As I have said, I was the one that Gauhar Mirza tormented most of all, and in spite of all the beatings he took from the maulvi his teasing went on for years. Finally we made our peace, or to put it more accurately, I got used to his tricks.

There was not much difference in our ages. He might have been a couple of years older than me. At the time of which I am speaking, I was about thirteen, and he was probably in his fifteenth year.

At this stage, I started to enjoy his teasing. He had a fine voice, and being the son of a *domni,* had a natural ear for rhythm and melody. He was an expert mimer, and when he performed he would throb in every vein. For my part I had become quite an accomplished singer. When the maulvi was out of the room, we would have great fun together. I would sing and he would mime; or he would sing and I would keep time. The older girls were crazy about his voice, and he was invited into all their rooms. On those occasions my presence was also necessary, because without my accompaniment his performance would lack its usual lustre. Amir Jan was especially fond of his singing. You must remember her, Mirza Sahib.

I said that I did not, and pressed her to go on with the account.

Amir Jan's best days were those when she served Mufakkhar ud Daula Bahadur. Then she was very young, and what a shapely, youthful figure she cut. You probably remember the song:

As fair as lotus blossom was her face;
Childish innocence, bewitching grace.

Coquette! She stole mens' hearts with cunning lies;
The wrath of God flashed in her slanting eyes.

She was slight in stature with a perfectly moulded frame; such slender hands and feet!

Here Umrao broke off her story for a while, and began to chat about Amir Jan.

'Ah yes,' I said. 'I saw her not so long ago. She's not worth hanging on a clothes-line now. She got so ugly, you can't bear to look at her.'

'Where did you see her?'

'In the house of that person—you know, where Shah Sahib used to stand wearing a red suit and holding a thousand-bead rosary in his hand. He would greet anyone who came out of the house, but would never ask any questions.'

'I understand. You mean that Shah Sahib who was one of her lovers. So you live, there, do you?'

'Let's say I'm one of the company.'

'And how is she?'

'She's mad about some doctor. But you wouldn't know him, even if I told you his name. So there's no point.'

'Go on. Tell me. I'll work it out.'

'You know the Nakkhas. . . .'

'I've got it. Well, at that time she was so striking that people couldn't take their eyes off her. She was very grand and thought very highly of herself. Let alone the common people, she wouldn't even entertain the prayers of the greatest. She acted the part as well. She would go around with four maids, one to carry her hookah, one her fan, another her water-pot, and the fourth carrying her pan-box. She also had liveried servants running behind her conveyance. And that was the Amir Jan who was mad about Gauhar Mirza's voice. She knew how to sing herself, of course, but preferred to listen. In his youth, that boy was the play-thing of the elder girls. They were all crazy about him. He had the sort of face that you could easily fall in love with. A bit on the dark side, but handsome features. On top of that he had charm, style, a sort of wickedness, impishness and. . . .'

'Not surprising, when you know who his mother was.'

'Aha! So you saw Banno as well.'

I smiled: 'Yes. You may assume that to be the case.'

'Mirza! You are a dark horse, hiding your secrets under a veil.'

'Well, you've torn the veil now.'

'All right. Let's relax for a moment. Consign my lifestory to the flames.'

'We've got all evening to relax. Carry on with your story.'

Umrao resumed her account:

'Up to about eleven in the morning, no one dared leave the maulvi's presence even for a moment. Then he went off for his lunch, and we were free to do as we pleased. At once we were in and out of every room. One day with Amir Jan, the next day in Jafari's room, the day after that with Battan. Wherever we went, there was a warm welcome—fruit, sweets, a hookah, pan. . .'

I again broke into the story: 'Did you start to smoke the hookah even as a child?'

'Yes. I first had the desire when I saw Gauhar Mirza smoking. At first, it was just for fun, and now it's turned into a wretched habit.'

'Gauhar Mirza used to smoke that strong opium. I shouldn't be surprised if you picked up that habit as well.'

'No. To this day the good Lord has preserved me from that. But I do confess to taking a little of the weaker variety. It started not so long ago when I returned from my pilgrimage to Karbala. I came down with a shocking cold when I was there and it turned to catarrh. The doctor advised it.'

'But what about that other stuff for stopping catarrh?'

'Don't mention it!'

'You mean, you've given it up.'

'Long ago.'

'I agree. That stuff is a curse. It's happened to me, you know.'

I repented, but the yearning still remains.
I swore, but still I crave the cup to ease my pains.'

'Mirza Sahib, what a fine verse! I am always rêady to extract oaths, but the decision to drink or not is up to you.'

'Well, perhaps you'll join me.'

'Good help me!'

'Me as well!'

The clouds have come; the cool, sweet breeze is blowing,
But where its memory leads us there's no knowing.'

'Mirza, calm yourself! For God's sake, lets drop the subject. I'm sorry I made the joke.

But now I shall not bring it to my lips;
I remembered. Well, then I remembered.'

'Umrao! What a fine verse!'

'Thank you.

They saw where martyrs fell, slain by her charms;
The red rose and the tulip they remembered.'

'By the grace of Allah! You are in form. But why not? This is the effect of recalling one's youth.'

'No. It is the effect of remembering the pleasures of wine!

Oh pious men! That very thing today
That caused our enmity I have remembered.'

'Ah, ah! What a verse! Excellent!

We left the Ka'ba and we went astray;
The temple's road was all that we remembered.'

'Well said, Mirza! "We left the *Ka'ba*"—that's a fine idea. But why don't you turn it into a first verse with a double rhyme. Something like this:

We left the Ka'ba; all that we remembered
Was on the temple's road. That we remembered.'

'Not bad. Do you have another?'
Umrao responded immediately:

'The garden and the birds' song we remembered;
It was the desert fall that we remembered.'

'That's quite good for a beginning as well.'
'Try this one:

We quarrel with the daughter of the vine;
But why without her gift have we remembered?'

'Umrao! I repeat, you are excelling yourself today. Hear just one more verse, then continue with your story:

Let there be the breeze, the cloud, the garden and the wine;
But let there be that sweet past youth for which we ever pine.'

'Ah, Mirza. You capture my heart. But let me get on with

my tale:

I spent several years at Khanum's house in the way I have described. During that time nothing special happened that I need to mention. But there is one thing that is worth mentioning. Bismillah's 'inauguration,' which we call *missi,* * was celebrated in great style. I have never seen anything so grand from the royal period to this day. The Dilaram summer-house was adorned for this function. Inside and out, the place was flooded with light. Not only were male and female singers, Kashmiri jesters and dancers brought from the city, but itinerant courtesans were also invited from far and wide. Singers of the highest reputation were sent for, even from as far away as Delhi, and the singing and dancing went on for seven days and nights. People still talk of the generosity displayed by Khanum. Of course, Bismillah was Khanum's only child, and no expense was spared.

Nawab Chabban had inherited a fortune from his grandmother, Nawab Umdat ul Khaqan Begum. He was a very young prince, and God only knows the tricks Khanum played to ensnare him. But the poor fellow was caught and parted with almost thirty thousand at that function. After that, Bismillah remained in the Nawab's service, and he loved her to distraction.

"Mirza Sahib! I do find it very difficult to answer all your questions. It is true that prostitutes are known for their candid speech, but there is a time and a place for everything. It is all a matter of one's age. Things that are said with exaggeration in the first flush of youth should lose their significance with passing years, and a kind of balance should be struck. After all, prostitutes are women as well. But what do you get out of asking me all these details?'

I answered her question:

'There is some advantage in my insistence. If you were not educated, then I would give some consideration to your objections, but people like us have no need for modesty and shame in such matters.'

'You mean that education shields you from modesty.'

'All right, all right! But go on. Let's not waste time with irrelevant detail.'

'I hope you are not going to publish this in some newspaper.'

'What do you think?'

'Ah, the disgrace! God preserve us! Will you make me as notorious as yourself? The very pen-name you've chosen is a word meaning "disgraced."'

'Well, if you share my notoriety, that's no crime.'

'God help anyone who ever falls in love with you!

Converse with pious preachers and argue with the wise;
Nothing comes of anything, till someone's name is said.'

'Whose verse is that?'

'Why do you ask me?'

'I see. But tell me, did you also hear the poem?:

'I go to sell my soul upon the market place of love.
But ere I strike love's bargain, never more this path I'll tread.'

'And do you remember that verse which ended in "*till every stone is bled.*"

'Yes:

Be it a promise or a vow, my lover is so mean;
No one receives a thing from him till every stone is bled.'

'Anything else?'

'No, I can't recall any other lines.'

'That was a fine *ghazal.* If ever you find a copy, please show it to me.'

'Couldn't you ask him for it?'

'I could go myself and write it down, but I doubt whether he would agree.'

'Well perhaps one day we could go together. Ah, here's another verse:

Although my reputation might be stained in this affair,
He'll not relent till my bad name throughout the world is spread.

And another:

My rivals have the appetite for making cruel demands;
In their hands even love to degradation will be led.'

'I also wrote a poem in that rhyme-scheme, but heaven knows what became of it. All I remember is the last verse:

Why do you sit with Rusva and try to test his love?
I swear I shall not let you go until your face is red.'

'That's very fine, Mirza, but all the more interesting for containing your disgraceful pen-name!'

'Don't mention my pen-name. By the kindness of the people who are kind to me, there are now several notorious Rusvas in this city. For no reason, people seem to have abandoned their own good pen-names and to have adopted mine. It is perhaps just as well that they don't know my real name, otherwise they would probably have adopted that also. But I don't mind. It's like the English custom, whereby fathers and sons have the same name. So they are all my spiritual sons. As my progeny increases, so my name will become even more famous. Anyway, you have delayed for long enough. You must continue the account I requested.'

'Rusva! You are forcing me. What disgraceful questions you ask!'

'Isn't it more disgraceful when women sing bawdy songs at weddings?'*

'Higher-class prostitutes don't sing bawdy songs any more in Lucknow. That's the job of *domnis,* though prostitutes have to sing them in villages, even in male company. But whether in the town or in the country, I still don't think that it's a good custom.'

'Well, its not bad just because you say so. I've seen with my own eyes just how much pleasure the most upright nobles of our society get out of slipping into the women's quarters and hearing those songs. They listen to their mothers and sisters, and grin from ear to ear. I sometimes wish we had never lived to see this day. And not to mention the scurrilous things that the most respectable ladies sing on wedding nights and the morning after. Still, let's leave this topic and get on with the story. I'm no national reformer to criticise these things!'

When Bismillah's *missi* cermony had taken place, and Khursid and Amir had been through the same process, I had a strange desire in my own heart. I noticed that after a particular ritual, about which I was totally ignorant, Bismillah became Bismillah Jan, and Khurshid became Khurshid Jan. They acquired a sort of boldness and air of freedom. They kept themselves apart, and seemed to look down on me. They began to laugh and joke with men, not showing the slightest reserve, and had separate rooms reserved for them. They had string-beds, and their floors were covered with spotless white sheets, on which huge pan-boxes, beauty-cases and spittoons were carefully arranged. Shining mirrors were attached to their walls along with pictures, and the ceilings were covered with cloths in which was hung a small chandelier. At the start of the evening, the two larger chandeliers were lit.

Each of the girls had two maids and two servants who attended to them with folded hands. Every day they would be visited by handsome young men of the aristocracy, who would sit with them taking the silver stem of the *hookah* between their lips. The girls would offer each one pan and fill their pipes for them. If they stood up, the men would cry out: 'In the name of Allah!.' When they walked, people would cast their eyes before their feet. As for them, they cared for no one, and everyone was a slave at their command. They had such authority that even if heaven and earth would move, their word was law. Why talk of their demands? Without being asked people would give their hearts to them, offer up their very spirit and sacrifice their souls. They would accept no one's gift, pay no heed to anyone's request, and were so unconcerned that if a man offered his life, they considered it of little worth. In their overweening pride, they would kick the Sultanate of the Seven Climes with their feet. One moment they would reduce you to tears; at another make you laugh for joy. They would pinch your breast and trample your heart under their heel; they would sulk at the slightest thing. People would coax them, beseech them with folded hands, but they would not even lift their head. People stared in admiration of their beauty. Thousands of eyes were upon them; people were dying with envy; and they purposely fed the flames of their jealousy. But they had nothing in their hearts but contempt. All was superficial. If some poor wretch was beguiled by them, they would at first pretend to be dying of love:

Today she speaks so tenderly and treats me with respect;
For whom is death intended? For myself or for my foe?

Let his enemies die! At last she killed him. Her heart grew cold. In his house there was moaning, weeping. She sat with her friends, laughing merrily.

Mirza Sahib! You know all these things better than I do, and could easily describe them yourself. But I am the only one who knows the true feelings of my own heart. The envy a woman can feel for another woman knows no bounds. Although I am ashamed to admit it, I wanted all their lovers to be mine, and all those who were mad about them to be mad about me. I could not bear their men to look at them, to be dying for them. I wanted them all to look at me and die for me. But the truth is that no one showed the slightest interest.

In her room, Bua Husaini had a small stove in front of which there were scattered two large pots, some badly coated brass plates, a copper pan, a griddle, plates and cups. In one corner were stored a pot of flour, a few varieties of lentils, salt and spices in various containers. Nearby were piled up bundles of firewood, tinder, a slab for grinding spices on—in other words, the whole contents of a lumber room might be found there. On the door over the stove, there were two nails. When she cooked, a lamp used to be suspended there. By her bed was a greasy board on which she placed the lamp when she had finished cooking. The lamp had a thin string wick, which hardly showed any light. Try as hard as you may, the flame would never get any higher. To add to the decoration of this room there were two net baskets, in one of which she stored onions, and in the other was a brass container for curry and lentils, and a cover for chapatties which were all destined for the maulvi. The onion basket was over the stove, and the provision bag, from which came a constant odour of cooked food, hung immediately above the place I slept. If I woke up suddenly, I would bang my head on the brass curry box.

In the morning till eleven o'clock, the maulvi's grammar and whip; in the evening till nine o'clock, the music-teacher's brow-beating and rod - that was the sum of my life. However, I did not stop my pranks.

In those days, I used to love to admire myself in the mirror. I was then fourteen years old. No sooner had Bua Husaini stepped out of the room, I would go to her box and take out her looking-glass. I would gaze at my reflection and compare myself to the other prostitutes. I could see nothing at all wrong with my face. Indeed, I thought I looked better than the others, though that was not really the case.

Once more I interrupted:

'You mean you thought you might be worse-looking than anyone else? Even now you are better than hundreds of others. At that time you must have been much more attractive.'

'Thank you, Mirza. You will pardon me, but I shall ignore your flattery, which is untimely and out of place. But I agree that I was of the same opinion. And that was the main trouble. In my heart of hearts, I would say to myself: "What is so wrong with me that no one pays me any attention?"

'That is impossible. People must have been looking at you. But, of course, you had not yet been through your initiation ceremony, or *missi*, as you call it. People were afraid of Khanum, and that's why no one dared speak to you.'

'That is probably the case, but how was I to know that?

When I looked at the other girls, I would blaze with envy; I refused to eat and drink; at night I could not sleep. When I arranged my hair, it was even worse, because I had no one to tie my plaits. Nawab Chabban would tie Bismillah's with his own hands, and when I saw that, it felt as if a snake had coiled round my breast. But whom did I have? Just Bua Husaini, and that was only when she was free. Otherwise, my hair hung down loose all day long, and I would walk around looking like a haystack. Finally I learned to tie my own plaits. The other girls changed their clothes three times a day; I had one change a week. They had embroidered suits; I had the same old silk pyjamas, satin scarf and lace blouse.

'When I changed my clothes, I always wanted to sit down with the men, and sometimes I used to wander into the rooms of Bismillah Jan or Amir Jan. But on some pretext I was always shown the door. They no longer wanted me to join them. They had their own pleasures, and none of them liked me to be around.

'Another reason for my being excluded from their company was that I had started to play up. I would point my thumb at them, make faces, try to pinch them, and even attempt to flirt with their men. Therefore they were not too happy with my presence.

'Mirza Sahib! When I felt like that, you can understand what a consolation Gauhar Mirza was to me. He spoke affectionately, we would tease each other, I regarded him as my 'lover,' and he loved me in return. When we went to school in the morning, he would always have a couple of oranges in his pocket, and slyly give them to me. One day he had managed to get a rupee which he passed on to me. During my lifetime I have received hundreds of thousands of rupees, but I have never had so much joy when I was given that first coin. Before that, I had been given money, but never a whole rupee. I kept it with me for a long time, first because I had nothing to spend it on, and second because if I had tried to spend it people would have asked me where I had got it. I now learnt to keep secrets—a clear sign that I was approaching the age of discretion."

6

ایک شاطر چور دل میرا چرا کر لے گیا
پاسباں کمبخت سب سوتے کے سوتے رہ گئے

A cunning thief came in and stole my heart,
While all the wretched watchmen were asleep.

It was the rainy season and the clouds were spread across the sky. The rain was coming down in torrents; thunder roared and lightning flashed. I was alone in Bua Husaini's room: she had gone with Khanum to see Haidar. Her lamp had gone out, and it was so dark that you could not see a hand in front of your face.

In the other rooms the usual parties were going on, and the whole house was echoing with singing and peals of laughter.

But I was alone in the dark, feeling sorry for myself and weeping. I was afraid of the storm and had put my head under the blanket: when it thundered, I thrust my fingers into my ears. In this state I fell asleep. Suddenly I felt someone gripping my hand. My heart almost stopped beating. I could not cry out, and finally I fainted.

The next morning there was an investigation, but the thief had left no trace. Khanum was sitting with a long face, and Bua Husaini was walking up and down mumbling. I remained silent, looking shifty. They got tired of asking me questions. If I had known, I might have told them.

'You mean, if you had known you might not have told them'

'Don't embroider my story. Just listen.'

'Whenever I think of Khanum's disappointment and Bua Husaini's miserable face. I can't help laughing.'

'Why shouldn't you? All their hopes had been dashed and you had all the fun.

'Their hopes had been dashed? You don't know Khanum. She was full of tricks, and kept the whole matter quiet, as if nothing had happened. She was very good at pouring oil on troubled waters. Now she looked around for a client who had more money than sense, and in the end she found one.

It happened that the son of a magistrate had arrived in Lucknow from British India to further his education. His late father, who had done very well for himself mainly from bribes and tokens of esteem, had left a large part of his property for his son to spend. When he reached Lucknow, he behaved himself for a time, but then became dazzled by the bright lights. He soon developed a taste for roaming around and a fondness for the piquant. His name was Rashid Ali, and when he began to compose poetry, he took the pen-name 'Rashid.'

A Lucknow *ustad* took him under his wing, and he became very proud of this pen-name.

His servants, who had accompanied him from his home town, called him Rakkhan Miyan, while the people of Lucknow started to call him 'Raja'. But he considered this name far too rustic. He became so mad about high-society life in Lucknow that later he styled himself 'Nawab Sahib'. When he first arrived, he had quite a bushy beard, but after getting a taste of the big city, he had it trimmed, then clipped, and then completely shaved off. The final shaving revealed a small, ugly face, but he considered himself handsome! He had a black complexion, pock-marks, a sort of turned up nose, a squat neck, tiny little eyes and the stature of a dwarf. I think that is a fair description, but he thought himself a second Joseph. He would spend hours in front of his mirror, twirling his moustaches so carefully that they came to resemble mice tails. He grew his hair long and had it curled. With this he wore a cornered-hat, a high-collared overcoat, and wide-ankled pyjamas. Dressed in this attire, he entered the apartments of courtesans.

First, he was very shrewd, and secondly, by the intervention of some worthy companions, he gained access to the most important rooms. His shrewdness soon developed into informality, and he would exchange risqué comments and witticisms even with Chuttan Jan, and Bagan. One day Husna playfully hit him with her slippers. He grinned like a Cheshire cat. Even so, he treated the mistresses of these houses with great respect. Any girl he had even one night's liaison with, he would greet her mistress in public audiences as 'Mother,' showing his reverence with a low bow. The main point of this was, of course, to show his friends that he had 'arrived'. He would regularly visit Khanum's establishment, and stay from eight in the evening until the small hours of the morning. He tried his hands at all the arts, and being well-practised in music, sang folk-songs while keeping time with himself. He could do all the actions and could play the tabla on his teeth. His friends use to send him up and extravagantly praise his verse, calling him the envy of Atish and Nasikh.* They dragged him off to mushairas and egged him on to read out his poetry. The whole gathering would go into an uproar. They would always put him on just before the comic poets who recited in the style of women, and people would laugh themselves hoarse. He was, of course, very pleased and took one bow after another.

Money arrived from home by the bucket-full. His mother, convinced that her poor son was studying hard and would return as a fully-fledged maulvi, sent him whatever he asked for. All the dandies, fops and scroungers of Lucknow flocked around him. This encouraged him all the more, and because of them his first steps towards me progressed to desire, his desire turned into passion, and his passion developed into madness. And that is when Khanum got hold of him. I remember very well how she used to say: 'No, sir! She is far too young for you.' But he would try to persuade her with his pleading. Finally the magic worked, and with the help of his 'friends' the bargain was struck for five thousand rupees. In order to collect the money, he had to go home for a few days, and without telling his mother he mortgaged two of his villages. He returned to Lucknow with over twenty thousand rupees, from which he handed Khanum five thousand in cash.

Khanum's accountant put the money into her flourishing treasury; Bua Husaini also stretched out her hand and received a gift of five hundred. The upshot was that I was given over to him, and for the six months that he remained in Lucknow, he paid me a regular hundred a month without my ever having to ask for it. Everything I earned was secretly passed on to Bua Husaini, and Khanum was never informed of our deal. Now I was almost independent, and I was allotted two maids and two servants. I had a room by the gate for my accommodation, where several men, including sons of Nawabs, would come to sit with me.

The 'first to pluck the rose,' Gauhar Mirza, frequently saw me at that time. Khanum and Bua Husaini were furious, but since I loved him, there was nothing much they could do about it. In the meantime, Gauhar Mirza's father died, and so his source of income dried up. Banno was now getting on, and no one cared for her. Therefore I became responsible for Gauhar Mirza's expenses.

All courtesans, as a rule, keep a man for themselves, and derive many benefits from him. The first thing is that when there is no one else around, he at least provides pleasant company. There are no problems with shopping. If you order food from someone else, you get something, but your man will take special pains to scour the city for the very best. If you fall ill, you always get the finest treatment, all that you need for relaxation, and he will massage your legs all night long. He will run for medicine in the morning, give the doctor precise instructions, inform your friends and acquaintances, bring you herbs and powders. Whenever there is a wedding, he will take the responsibility of arranging a performance for you. In social gatherings he will draw peoples' attention to you. When you dance and sing, he will keep time for you, praise every note loudly, extol every modulation, explain every movement of the mime. Through his good offices, you get the best to eat, and are treated with much more courtesy than the other girls. On top of that you are given prizes and awards. If you happen to meet an aristocrat or a noble, he is very good at making them just that little bit jealous. The noble wants the girl to love him and him alone; the girl, however, praises her man to the skies. You begin with the sentence: 'Your honour, I belong to him; I don't think I should meet you. He will be coming home shortly. I think you'd better go now. After all, he is mine for ever. You could never be that.'

Your man has influence over your clients, and if there is any bother, he is always ready to help out. He knows all the wastrels and scoundrels of the city, and can round up fifty or sixty men with a snap of his fingers. The client also has some control over the mistress of the house, who is always afraid that her girl might fall in love and run away with him.

Amir Jan was once mad about Kazim Ali and for years he was in her pay. Once she gave him a pair of bangles worth five hundred rupees, and the next day made a hue and cry, telling everyone that they had been stolen. On another occasion, she gave him a pair of pearl ear-rings and said that she had dropped them at the fair in Aish Bagh. In this way she gave him thousands, all of which with he used to feed his family.

Khurshid fell for Pyare Sahib. Bismillah, however, had no one like this. She was by nature on the stingy side, and would give herself to no one.

Not to mention the others, Khanum Sahib herself, even when she was over fifty, fell in love with a boy of about nineteen, called Mir Aulad Ali. He had a young face and a well-built frame, and girls from the very best families had their eyes on him. But Khanum was a force to be reckoned with and no one dared to open their mouths before her. The poor fellow had no money and depended on Khanum for his daily bread. She in fact provided for his whole family. On his wedding she spent two and half thousand rupees, but apart from the first night of his honeymoon, Amir was not allowed to sleep in his home again. He kept Khanum company day and night, and she let him out only for a couple of hours a day to attend to his household affairs.

There was another Mirza Sahib, who must have been well over seventy. He was bent and did not have one tooth in his head. He was one of Khanum's old flames, and although he no longer had any status, he still lived like one of the family. Morning and evening, he ate with Khanum. She had his clothes made for him and paid for his opium, sugar and sweets.

One day we were all sitting with Khanum, and Khurshid Jan was looking miserable.

'What's the matter?,' enquired Khanum. 'Just because Pyare Sahib's got married, she's taking it so badly. I don't understand the girls of these days, and their petty affairs. They're as bad as their lovers. But in our day. . . Just look at him!' She pointed to Mirza. 'I had an affair with him when I was very young. His parents had arranged his marriage, and he came to show himself to me dressed up in his wedding-suit. I dragged the suit off his back and tore it to shreds. I sat him down and told him straight that I would never let him go. That was forty years ago, and to this day, he's never been back home once. Can any of you say the same?'

We all hung our heads in shame.

I had danced and sung once at Bismillah's inauguration, but my first professional performance was at the wedding of Nawab Shujaat Ali Khan. That was a memorable occasion. How beautifully the Nawab's pavilion was decorated! The priceless glass chandeliers turned night into day; the brilliant white ground-sheet, the Persian carpets, the cushions and bolsters embroidered with gold thread, and the rows of glittering lamps.

The perfume and scent of the flowers turned the pavilion into a garden, and the smell of the hookahs and areca nuts made one feel quite light-headed. I was about fourteen at the time, and a Gujarati singer had arrived from Baroda. Her fame had spread far and wide and the greatest of our singers touched their ears in reverence. Her knowledge was so vast that she seemed to have learned all the text-books by heart. Her voice had bewitched the whole city. But just see how cunning Khanum was. She put me on straight after her. I, of course, had no idea what was going on, but the connoisseurs were amazed. 'What chance does this little thing stand after Bai Ji's performance?' they said.

The first notes were struck and the whole audience turned towards me. I was in first blush of youth, and although I may not have been a ravishing beauty, I had a certain childish wickedness, cunning and innocent allure:

Do not ask me of the time of youth;
What can I say? It was a magic age.

I danced for a while, and Khanum asked me to sing a particular ghazal:

Today in the assembly was the dazzle of her face;
Behold in just one moment what a miracle took place.

As soon as I sang this first verse the audience was in raptures. I added another with both lines rhyming in the same manner, and as I performed the actions, the whole crowd began to sway:

What lamentation ceases, she gives torture in its place;
And when the pain decreases then her anger joins the race.

The audience erupted. I continued:

Then her looks are downcast and she coyly drops her glance,
And once again the arrow misses, straying from the trace.

The effect was such that when I sang the next verse, anyone whose glance I caught could not look away:

In idol-worship no-one is so infamous as I;
I drop my head, ashamed to hear the mention of God's grace.

Just hear the next verse and try to imagine what an effect if might have on people with a romantic temperament:

In love how can one tell you the desires of the heart?
In dying too there's pleasure, though this pleasure may be base.

Then I sang the next verse:

I was wrong I did not want to show the way I felt;
And now if I should say a word, imagine the disgrace.

The whole audience now seemed to be in a state of ecstasy. Everyone was overjoyed and cheered every word I sang. I had to repeat each verse eight or ten times. Even then they could not have enough. This *ghazal* marked the end of my performance. In the second round I was asked to sing it again.

Here I broke into her story and asked her if she could remember any more verses of the same poem. 'By the way,' I said. 'Who composed it?'

'Need you ask?' she replied. 'Listen to some more:

Those caught in the throes of death come closest to the grave;
But only when they've suffered all the pains of love's embrace.'

'By the grace of God,' I exclaimed.

'Whoever wrote it must have broken the pen!' she remarked.

If the sigh has one effect, it must be that of fire;
For otherwise the flame is wind and dies without a trace.

'That's philosophy,' I said. Whoever wrote it must have understood the science well.' She continued:

I incline in some way to the law of opposites;
My heart is only happy when its grieving runs apace.

'Philosophy again,' I said. 'Now I *know* the writer understands it. Is there more?'

If you wish to show yourself, then please don't break my heart;
For in its very mirror you for ever show your face.

'This is mysticism. We are people of the world and have no part of it. But "wish to show yourself"—why do you put the words together like that?'

'This is the last verse:

This night of separation, do not moan for poor. . .
For when that cruel one hears such cries, her anger joins the race.

'You have gone back to the first verse again. Did you not have time to compose. . . I mean recite the final verse including the pen name?'

Umrao resumed her account without comment.

A few days after my first performance, Bua Husaini entered my room with a servant. She introduced him and left the room. The gentleman touched his forehead and said:

'I have a message from Nawab Sultan Sahib, who yesterday was seated on the right side of the bridegroom wearing a yellow turban. He has asked if he might visit you at a time convenient to you, but wishes no one else to be present. He would also like to have copy of the poem you sang.'

I answered: 'Give my humble respects to the Nawab Sahib, and request him to come at any time that suits him in the evening. He will have complete privacy. You may call for the poem at any time tomorrow. I shall write it out for you.'

The next day during the late morning the servant arrived. I was alone in my room, and gave him a copy of the poem, he gave me five ashrafis,* saying that the Nawab knew that such a small sum was not worthy of me, but begged me to accept it towards the expense of my pan. He would be with me that evening at the time of the lighting of the lamps.

The servant bowed and left. My first though was to call Bua Husaini and show her the gold coins and ask her to give them to Khanam. Then I looked again at the glittering, newly minted money, and thought the better of it. Since I had no money-box of my own. I hid them under the foot of the bed.

Mirza Sahib! In my opinion there comes a time in every woman's life when she wants someone to love her. Please do not imagine that this is a passing fancy, but it is a desire which begins with the onset of youth and grows stronger with the passing years.

There can be no doubt that Gauhar Mirza was my lover, but his affection was different. There was something lacking in his love, something I sought but did not obtain. He had no manly strength in his character, and he had inherited the temperament of his mother. Whatever he found he snatched away from me and kept it for himself. Apart from that one rupee I mentioned, he never gave me anything else. I was now looking for a lover who would pander to my every whim, spend fortunes on me, regale me with banquets. Nawab Sultan was such a man. He was good looking and had the firmness in his features by which any woman might be beguiled. Some people mistakenly believe that all a woman wants is flattery and superficial declarations of love. That, of course, is important but it is also necessary that there should be no meanness, no ulterior motive. There are men who come to admire a courtesan's jewels, but who with every gesture betray their real purpose: 'Love me! For God's sake, love me! Come and live in my house; give me all you have; take over the running of my home; cook my meals; attend to the needs of my children.' Not every man can boast the miraculous beauty of Joseph and expect any woman to fall head over heels in love with him. Men and women do love each other, but in love there is often an element of self-interest. Selfless love, like that of Laila and Majnu, Shirin and

Farhad, only exists in tales. People say that love cannot be one-sided. I have seen even this with my own eyes, but I think we must regard it as a kind of aberration. And why should it be necessary for men and women to be crazy?

The next day the Nawab came as promised. He exchanged a few formal words with Bua Husaini, settled his account and entered the privacy of my room. I found out that he had not arranged for a servant: he had fixed it that he would come occasionally for an hour or two at night. He was a simple man of few words, only nineteen years old, and had been brought up, as we say, under the dome of sanctity. He had been protected by his parents and was totally innocent of the deceits of the world. He had delivered his 'declaration of love' through a servant, and would have found it difficult to do so by himself. But I soon put him at his ease.

I told him many words of love, and showed him how I wept for him. Some of what I said was true, and some utterly false. True, because the Nawab had the kind of features that would attract the most hard-hearted woman. He was fair, and his complexion was like a rose; his features were classic; his forehead high; his eyes were bright and the biceps rippled on his arms. He had broad wrists and a tall muscular frame. It was as if God had bathed his body from head to foot in the mould of divine light. Along with this, his speech was innocent, interspersed with amorous verses, most of which were of his own composition, and when he recited poetry he would be quite bold. He was from a family of poets, and had often attended mushairas with his father.

Most poets, no matter how amorous or bold the verse, will recite it before anyone without a trace of embarrasment. The young in front of the elderly, the elderly in front of the young, though in normal circumstances they would be on their guard, lose all their inhibitions when they recite poetry. There are many things you can express in verse that you would never dare to utter in prose. In short, that evening passed in the most enjoyable way. The Nawab began the conversation:

'Your charms so beguiled me that without seeing you I could not rest.'

'It is all due to your generosity, otherwise what am I?

Ayaz qadr-e khud bishanas; man danam ki man anam
Ayaz, know thy place; I know what I am.'*

'So you know Persian?'

'Yes, a few words.'

'Can you write as well?'

'Yes. A little.'

'So this poem was written in your hand.'

I smiled and let the Nawab continue.

'By Allah! What charming handwriting. I really am so glad. Communicating through servants is not quite the same thing. From now on I shall write to you the feelings of my heart. This is just as I wanted it. As far as possible it is better to avoid the intercession of strangers:

We'll let no strangers interfere;
No friends our joys or pains shall see.
The words that pass between ourselves
Belong to only you and me.'

'Is that your verse?'

'No, one of my father's.'

'It is very well said.'

'Praise be to Allah! You appreciate poetry as well:

God has bestowed a lovely face.
But let Him give these qualities:
The gift of speech to charm the ear.
A pretty hand to charm the eyes.

That is also one of his verses. He wrote well and his lines are fitting only for your magnificence.'

'Thank you, Nawab Sahib:

But all is due to your kind grace;
For what am I? Where is my place?'

'That is fine verse. Do you compose poetry as well?'

'No, no. I have it composed by kind patrons like yourself.'

When he heard these words the Nawab looked a little confused; then he smiled and his smile turned to laughter. 'I see,' he said. 'I have heard that most courtesans have their verse composed by friends, and then recite them in their own name.'

'Only courtesans? Do not other people do the same thing?'

'By God, that is true! My late father had many friends who had never composed a line in their lives, but they always had a *ghazal* ready for a *mushaira*. But what satisfaction can there be in receiving false praise for someone else's work?'

'I don't know. It is a kind of greed. A disreputable emotion.'

'Still, it happens. If you know another verse from that *ghazal,* please recite it.'

'You try to tame your heart's lament;
But why such wrath, if that's the case?'

'What a fine verse!' Recite it again. You have said something quite new.'

I recited it again, but when he requested more verses, I had to admit that no others existed. I had just made them up on the spur of the moment.

'That is marvellous,' he replied. 'Impromptu verse, and of such high quality!'

I asked him to recite some of his own verse, and he was just on the point of doing so when the door burst open. A man of about fifty was standing there. He was dark with a bushy beard; his turban was awry and in his belt he carried a dagger. He barged his way into the room and very rudely sat down placing his hand on my knee. The Nawab looked at me and I lowered my eyes; you could have struck me down dead. I had promised the Nawab complete privacy, and now as we were enjoying our conversation, our discreet jokes and our dalliance, this thunderbolt from the blue crashed down upon us. Our evening had been ruined by this uncouth wretch. The Nawab was just about to recite his poem; I would have responded with one of my own. How joyfully I would have accepted his praises. Here was the person my heart had been seeking for ages. And now everything was in tatters. 'Please God! Get him out of here,' I prayed, but all I saw before me were his bloodthirsty looks, which made my whole body shudder. It was as if Dilavar Khan had returned to haunt me. All the time, I feared that he might take out his dagger and plunge it into my breast, or, worse still, do harm to the Nawab. In my heart, I cursed him to hell. Why on earth had this disaster befallen me?

Finally in desparation I called out for Bua Husaini. She hurried in and immediately realised what was going on. It appeared from her conversation that she knew the person slightly. She addressed him:

'Listen to me, Khan Sahib. Please leave at once.'

'If you've got anything to say, say it here. When I sit down, I don't get up.'

'Khan Sahib! Are you going to use force?'

'What do you mean "force"? This is a whore-house, isn't it? No one has a monopoly. And if I have to use force, I will. We'll see who can make me get up!'

'Yes, there is a monopoly. It belongs to those who pay good money. No one else has right to come.'

'All right. I'll pay.'

'No, it is not convenient now. Please come another time.'

I could see the Nawab's face turning red with anger, but so far he had not said a word. Bua Husaini turned to me:

'My dear, just go out for a while. Nawab Sahib, it's time for your rest.

Please go to the other room.'

I began to rise, but the ruffian caught me by the arm, and I was powerless. The Nawab now addressed him:

'Khan Sahib! Leave the girl alone. It will be better for you if you go. You are behaving very badly. So far I have been silent, because I think it unseemly to brawl in such an establishment. But now. . .'

'But now what? We'll see what. . . is going to leave her alone.'

I screamed out: 'Please let go of my hand!'

Khan Sahib let go and the Nawab spoke firmly:

I tell you to moderate your language. You have obviously never kept company with men of honour.'

'And I suppose you have,' bawled Khan Sahib. 'So what are going to do about it?'

'Obviously you are spoiling for a fight, but the house of courtesan is neither a wrestling arena nor a field. You had better leave it for another time, otherwise. . .'

'Otherwise, you will melt me down and drink me. Go yourself!'

'Khan Sahib, excuse me. I've given you every opportunity, simply because I have some self-respect and consideration for my parents, relations and friends, otherwise I would make you laugh on the other side of your face for your impudence. Once more, I tell you not to waste your time arguing. Please leave. I beg of you.'

'Ah, so that's it. You come to a whore-house, and are afraid to tell mummy and daddy. What impudence are you talking about? Am I your old man's servant or something? Be a little prince in your own home if you want. But what it all boils down to is that you're sitting in a whore-house, and I'm sitting in a whore-house. I'll go when I want and not before. So it's you who are wasting your time arguing. No one's going to make me get up.'

There's no problem in having you thrown out. All I have to do is to call my men. They'll take you out by the scruff of the neck.'

'I wouldn't rely on servants if I were you. Have you seen this knife?'

'Yes, I've seen many like it. But the most effective knife is the one that works. I've already taken the size of your neck. We'll see who wins.'

'Come on, young fellow! You better go home. Mummy and daddy will be wondering where you are.'

The Nawab's face now changed completely. He was shaking with rage, but still managed to control himself. The miserable oaf had insulted him vilely but he tempered his tongue. First of all, I thought he was afraid, but I was wrong. The Nawab was really thinking of his own dignity was, and for that reason was giving ground. I wanted the matter to be dealt with calmly, but the stupid man's speech grew more wicked. The more leeway the Nawab gave him, the bolder he became. Finally the Nawab said:

'Right, get up Khan Sahib! We'll leave quietly and go to the park in Aish Bagh. There we'll settle the matter between us.'

Khan Sahib roared with laughter: 'Look, sonny! You're still wet behind the ears, and you talk about fighting with real men. If you get grazed, mummy will cry her heart out.'

The Nawab shouted: 'You bastard! You've gone too far now. I'll show you what you get for your impudence.'

With that the Nawab pulled his hand out of his quilted jacket and brandished a pistol. He fired and Khan Sahib fell down with a thud. I went numb as I saw blood spreading over the carpet. Bua Husaini was rooted to the ground. Hearing the sound of the pistol, Khanum, Mir Sahib, Khurshid, Amir Jan and Bismillah Jan all piled into the room. They were all speaking at once. Shamsher Khan, a middle-aged man in the Nawab's retinue, rushed into the room and took the pistol from the Nawab's hand.

'Now, sir, please go home. I'll sort it out.'

'No,' cried the Nawab. 'I shall not leave. What happened has happened and I'll face the consequences.'

Shamsher Khan, taking a dagger from his belt, said: 'I swear by the Lord, if you do not leave, I shall plunge this dagger into my breast. You must not stay now.'

Meanwhile Khan Sahib had been examined and we saw that the bullet had only entered his arm. His life was not in danger.

Shamsher Khan once again pleaded with the Nawab to preserve his dignity and leave, and finally persuaded him to do so. He left in the company of one of our men. Khanum sent for the local policeman, Mirza Ali Beg, who happened at that moment to be in the Chowk. She took him aside and whispered something in his ear. He understood and instructed us to take Khan Sahib downstairs, and assured us that the matter would be sorted out.

We did as he said, bandaged the arm and ordered a sedan. Khan Sahib recovered consciousness, and we found out that he lived in the Chicken Market. The bearers were told to take him home and return at once.

For several days, neither Sultan Sahib nor any of his men came to the house. I had fallen in love with him and was certain I would never see him again. This turned out to be true for a while. He was a man of impeccable habits, and from the very start he had insisted that our meetings should be held in strict privacy. Bua Husaini had done her best to respect his wishes, but it had not occurred to her to station someone near the door. Khan Sahib had arrived like a demon from hell, and now everything was spoilt.

After a week or so, I happened to have a wedding engagement. When I arrived for my performance, I noticed Nawab Sultan sitting among the guests. I was due on stage on nine o'clock. There was no question of my talking to the Nawab; it was even impossible to communicate through sign language. I spotted a fair boy of about nine years old wearing a heavy coat, who was sitting next to Nawab Sultan. I finished my performance, and when I had changed my clothes in the private room, I beckoned to him. I offered him a *pan* and asked him if he knew Sultan.

'Which Sultan?'

'The one who was sitting near you opposite the groom.'

He frowned: 'He's my elder brother. How dare you call him Sultan!'

'Very well. If I give you something, will you pass it to him?'

'He won't be angry?'

'No, of course not.'

'What are you giving him? *Pan?'*

'No, no. I'm sure he's got plenty with him. Just hand him this piece of paper.'

There happened to be a piece of paper lying on the ground. I took some charcoal and wrote:

So long am I deprived of his reproach;
Today in the assembly shall I tease him?

I told the boy to place, the paper in front of him without his seeing it, and the boy did as he was told. Sultan Sahib picked up the paper. At first, he looked a little anxious, but when he read it, he smiled and put it in his pocket. Calling Shamsher Khan, he whispered something in his ear. Within an hour, Shamsher came to my room to tell me the Nawab would send me a written reply the next day.

My next performance took place in the morning, but Sultan Sahib had left the party. Without his presence there was no life in the gathering, and I had little inclination to sing. Somehow or other, I got through my act and went home, where I eagerly awaited Shamsher's arrival. He came in the early evening and gave me the Nawab's note, which read as follows:

'Your verse rekindled in my heart the fire which had burnt low. I really do love you, but am constrained by honour. I shall never again be able to set foot in your house. I have a close friend who lives in Navaz Ganj. I shall invite you there tomorrow. Please come if you are free. This is one way of meeting, and we shall be undisturbed until ten in the evening.

Why regret the passing of the night we met?
Here I grow impatient just for one more glance.'

From that day onwards, Nawab Sultan never set foot in Khanam's house. Two or three times a week, he summoned me to Nawab Banne Sahib's house in Navaz Ganj. We had such pleasurable times. Sometimes we would read poetry; sometimes Nawab Banne Sahib would accompany my singing on the tabla. Sultan Sahib would also sing. He knew little of rhythm and melody, but sung his own verse not too badly:

The practice of exchanging glances grows;
I look at her and she returns my glance.

I can still picture those meetings. The hot evenings, the moon riding the sky, the white cloth spread in the garden where we would sit, the comfortable bolsters on which we would recline, everything of luxury to hand; the garden with its varied blossoms, the senses overwhelmed by the scent of jasmine, the sweet-smelling *pan* leaves, bubbling hookahs, our informal dalliance in complete privacy.

As we sat together, nothing in the world mattered to us. We might even forget that God existed. For this sin our punishment was that these pleasures passed away too soon, leaving us to regret them for the rest of our days, even perhaps after death:

Why ask the pleasures of the pain of love?
I even thought of them in Paradise.

Sultan and I were truly in love. We shared the same humour so exactly that we could have enjoyed each others' company for the whole of our lives. Sultan Sahib loved poetry, and I too have loved it since my early childhood. I have never felt closer to anyone than I felt with him, and I believe he loved me for the same reason. At the slightest pretext he would recite verses and I would cap them:

When stars and moon were forced apart, the heart cried out:
'So many ruined nights of joy before me lie.'

I teased Umrao for a moment: 'That is true! Many nights of joy have been ruined by your arrival.'

'Really, Mirza Sahib. My enemies are hovering around. That's a fine thing to say!'

'No, I don't mean it like that, but it's true. Whenever you come along, the whole gathering is finished.'

'Say what you like. If I had known you were going to speak in this way, I would never have agreed to tell you my story. But the harm's done now.'

'Harm? But this is the first thing you have done in your life to make your name immortal. I can't say whether it will bring you fame or infamy, and I take no responsibility for that. But let's leave the matter for now. Recite a few more verses of that *ghazal,* if you can remember them.'

'You really know how to set people up.'

'Yes, but I at least don't bring them down. Recite.'

'Very well. Here is the first verse and two others:

The heartache's joy was spent in nights of grief; the sigh
In separation lost its force and grief passed by.

and:

And when she sat in tears, her tresses hanging loose,
All my desires were partners in her doleful cry.

Companions! See what omens loom o'er our last tryst;
Our meeting started, then 'twas time to say goodbye.'

During that time, I entered the service of Nawab Jafar Ali Khan. He was about seventy year old, completely toothless, his back was bent and he did not have one black hair left on his head, but he still thought himself worthy of love. I'll never forget his snake-skin over-garment, satin pyjamas with the red sash, and his lace hat from underneath which his ringlets dropped.

You might wonder why anyone of that age and in such a physical state should find it necessary to keep a prostitute in his pay. But, listen, Mirza Sahib. It was a fashion in those days, and most aristocrats did the same thing. In the Nawab's administration, apart from the other trappings of elegance and power, there was a special place reserved for a courtesan, who would receive a salary of seventy-five rupees a month. Her function was to pray for his well-being. She only had to spend two hours in his company, and was then free to go home. The Nawab was now old and would never entertain people in his dining room after nine in the evening. If the diners happened to be late, he would go and dismiss them himself. His mother was still alive and he feared her like a five year old child. He also had great affection for his wife, to whom he had been married in his childhood. Apart from the first ten days of Muharram, he never slept apart from her.

You might laugh at me, but you can trust to my experience. He was certainly quite capable of making love, and when he sang the dirges for the death of Husain, known as *soz,** you would be transfixed. He was an expert musician and had no equal in singing. He had been known to correct the best performers, and in the art of *soz* he was without a rival. When

I served him, I profited greatly from his knowledge, and learned hundreds of dirges. For this I became known far and wide.

The ceremony for the mourning of Husain, organized by Khanum, was one of the finest in the city. During the first ten days of the month of Muharram, she would have a daily gathering, and on the tenth day would provide food for hundreds of poor Shi'as. Every Thursday up to the fortieth day she would hold a *majlis.** My ability to sing dirges was well-known, and no one knew more of the finer points of the art than I. Even the greatest masters did not dare open their mouths in my presence, and it was for this reason that I gained access to the court of Nawab Malika Kishvar. Every Muharram, I received much attention also from the royal circle. I also excelled in the art of the elegy,* and in the evening, after having performed my lamentation in the Imambara, I was obliged to stay at the palace door until two in the morning.

At the time when Bismillah's initiation-ceremony took place, Nawab Chabban's uncle, whom they called the Elder Nawab, had gone to make his pilgrimage to Karbala, from where he returned after about six months. His daughter was engaged to Nawab Chabban, and when the uncle returned home, he insisted on the marriage taking place. Now the Nawab was mad about Bismillah Jan. She had suggested that she might go to live in his house. The Nawab refused point blank to marry his cousin, but during the royal period you can imagine the reaction. He had badly insulted a girl of the aristocracy.

One evening there was a party in the Nawab's house. All his friends were gathered there, and Bismillah was sitting at the Nawab's side. I was singing and the Nawab was playing the tanpura, while one of his special guests, Dilbar Husain, was beating the tabla. In the meantime, a messenger came to announce the arrival of the Nawab's uncle. He thought that the elder Nawab would go up to see the Begum Sahib, Nawab Chabban's mother, and we all thought the same. But instead, he came straight into the living room where we were assembled. Seeing the party in full swing, he flew into a rage, and that put a stop to our singing. The Nawab stood up in deference, but his uncle ignored him.

'Leave the formalities and ceremonies. I have something important to say to you.'

The Nawab begged him to speak.

'You are a child, and do not know that my younger brother, the late Ahmad Ali Khan, died before his late mother. Therefore, you are excluded from the inheritance, and have no rights on the property to which at present you lay claim and of which you are enjoying the proceeds. No doubt his mother named you as her son, and until her dying day mentioned your name in her will. But that means nothing. According to the will, all you can receive is on third of the estate. From all accounts, it would appear that you have already had more than the third due to you. Anyway, I have no claim on your third, and since you are my flesh and blood, I shall not press you on what you have spent over and above that sum.'

At this point the elder Nawab's eyes flooded with tears, but he controlled himself and continued:

'You could have enjoyed the whole of this estate for the rest of your life. My own personal fortune is enough for my needs, and you would even have inherited that. But your bad behaviour leaves me with no alternative but to cut you off from the estate which you might have inherited. What your ancestors justly earned is not there to be wasted by such scoundrels as you. Munsif ud Daula's men are on my side. You and your scrounging friends can depart at this moment.'

Nawab Chabban was dumbfounded: 'You mean I have no right to the property?'

'Not a penny!'

'But you said I have a right to a third.'

'You have had that. If you think you still have any claim, go to court. But I think it unlikely that you will get anything.'

'Very well, but I shall take my mother with me.'

'She has already washed her hands off you. She will go to Karbala with me.'

'But where shall I go?'

'How do I know? You better ask your friends, your servants, your mistress!'

'Very well, but at least let me have my clothes and personal things.'

'Nothing in this house belongs to you. Not even the clothes you stand up in.'

In the meantime, the magistrate's men entered the house and proceeded to throw the Nawab and his company out.

We also left and hired a palanquin to take us to the Chowk. God alone knows where the Nawab and his friends went. Later, we heard that his friends abandoned him. While he was wandering in the streets, he happened to meet one of his father's old servants whom, sometime before, he had dismissed from his service as useless. The old man took pity on his former master and asked him to come home with him.

After we got home, Bismillah had a party in her room. Who should turn up but Miyan Hasnu, one of the Nawab's bosom friends, who had often sworn to lay down his life and shed his blood on the very spot where the Nawab's sweat should fall. Before, he would come stealthily in case the Nawab found out, but today there he was sitting quite openly, as large as life, displaying all his finery. Now he acted quite informally with

Bismillah Jan, and began to talk about her entering his own service:

'Look, Bismillah Jan. You can have no further hope of the Nawab. I'll give you whatever you ask. I'm a poor man, and don't have much to spare, and obviously cannot pay you even half of what you received from the Nawab. But all the same, I'll make you happy.'

Bismillah sneered at him: 'You, poor? You don't say how you milked the Nawab and filled your own coffers. Then you plead poverty. If they melted you down you would yield more than a hundredweight of fat!'

Hasnu protested: 'Now that's going too far. You say I milked the Nawab, but do you think my mother was worthless?'

'Your mother? Wasn't she Bua Farkhanda, one of Nawab Sarfaraz's maids?'

Hasnu looked sheepish: 'What's that got to do with it? When she died, she left me jewels worth four thousand rupees.'

'Yes, I know. But your wife took them when she ran off with her lover! What did you have left? Don't try it on with me. I know more about you than you think.'

'Well then, what about my father? He was well-off.'

'He was one of Nawab Hasn Ali Khan's fowlers.'

'Fowlers?'

'Sorry! Cock-fighters.'

'Cock-fighters?'

'All right. Gamekeepers. I know he had something to do with birds.'

'Now you're making fun of me.'

'I speak my mind, and hence I have a bad reputation. And why shouldn't I speak out? I get fed up with your boasting. When you used to come before, I didn't object, but the very moment the Nawab's fortune changed, you have the cheek to ask me to my face to "enter your service"!

Shake your brains. How could you keep anyone. Even if you did, it wouldn't last more than a couple of months.'

'Shall I give you six months' pay in advance?'

'With your mouth!'

'Well, take this.'

Hasnu pulled two jewelled bracelets from his pocket. 'How much do you think they're worth?'

Bismillah took them and put them on her wrists: 'I'll show them to Channa Mal's boy tomorrow. They look quite well made. But you'd better go now. I have an appointment with Chuttan Baji, and can't wait. Come the same time tomorrow.'

'Well, let me have my bangles back then.'

'Do you think you're dealing with thieves? I'm not going to eat your bangles. Look, I've only got plain ones on my arms. If I go and ask mother, she'll want to know where I'm going. So let me keep them just for this evening. I'll give them back tomorrow.'

'No. Let me have them back now. They're not mine. Otherwise, of course you could have them.'

'What? Are they your mother's? But she's dead. They must belong to you.'

'No, I just wanted to show them to you. They're not mine.'

'As if I didn't know. They're the bracelets the Nawab sent to be pawned when I was sitting there.'

'What do you mean? When?'

'The day he asked Umrao for a performance. She insisted on a hundred rupees, but the Nawab had no cash on him. In front of my eyes he took these bracelets out of his box and threw them down. Isn't that right, Umrao?'

I agreed and she carried on.

'Go and take a running jump! I shan't let you have them. They belong to the Nawab.

'But what about the money I gave you?'

'That also belongs to the Nawab.'

'But I got the interest from the money-lender.'

'Very well. Send for the money-lender and I'll pay him. On your way!'

'Well, at least let me have my bangles back.'

'No. I'm not parting with them.'

'That's force you're using.'

'Yes. Force! Now you'd better crawl out of here, otherwise...'

'All right. I'll come for them tomorrow.'

'We'll see.'

With these words, Bismillah gave him such a black look that he had no alternative but to go.

The fact of the matter is that Nawab Chabban's uncle had been through the accounts with his servants and had redeemed all the property by paying both capital and interest to whomsoever it was due. When Hasnu had been asked to account for the bracelets, he lied and said that he had not pawned them. That was his mistake.

As soon as Hasnu left, Bismillah explained:

'You can see how artful he is. He's brought ruin on the Nawab's house, and I've been waiting to catch him out for ages. Today he fell into my trap. You don't think I'm going to give him these bracelets back. They're stolen property.'

I agreed and suggested that she return them to the Nawab.

I'm not going to do that either. They're worth eleven hundred, and he got them for two hundred. I'll give him two-fifty, and that's my last offer.'

'But why did the money lender give that?'

'The money-lender paid the full sum. But when the Nawab

asked him, he went back on his word. If he makes any more fuss, I'll have him before the magistrate.'

As we were talking, the Nawab entered the house, looking glum. There were tears in his eyes. All his former grandeur and levity had gone. He sat down quietly.

To be truthful, I also had tears in my eyes, but you have to hand it to Bismillah. A typical prostitute! Immediately she embarked on the matter of the bracelets:

'You see these bracelets? They're the ones you gave Hasnu to pawn for you,' aren't they?'

'Yes, but he cheated me. I never got the money.'

'How much were they pawned for?'

'I don't know. A couple of hundred.'

'And the interest?'

'No one ever worried about interest before. I don't think we ever bothered to redeem anything.'

'Right. Can I have them?

'Yes. Take them.'

'If you like, I'll have Hasnu brought before the police.'

'No, please don't do that. He's a Sayyid. A descendant of the Prophet.'

'A Sayyid! You don't know his father.'

'Well, that's what he says.'

Secretly, I admired the Nawab's fortitude. But of course, he was from a noble family. But how heartless Bismillah Jan was. She made the same excuse about seeing Chuttan Jan, and sent the Nawab away.

A few days after this, I was sitting with Khanum, when an old lady entered the room. She bowed before Khanum and was offered a seat. The old lady explained her mission: 'I want to have a word with you in private. I wonder if. . .'

'Well, I'm here, you're here and there's only this girl. She hardly understands a thing. Please go on.'

'The lady, Nawab Fakhr un Nisa Begum, sent me.'

'Who is that?'

'You know, Nawab Chabban's. . .?

'I see. Please continue.'

'Well, the lady says that Nawab Chabban is her son, and she adores him as much as his late father did. She worships the ground he walks on, and his uncle does not dislike him either. He really treats him better than he treats his own children. He has an only daughter who is betrothed to Nawab Chabban. But Chabban has insulted her and refuses to marry her. His uncle insists and he has been properly admonished. As far as your daughter is concerned, she will be looked after for life. Whatever salary was fixed for her, you can have ten times that amount. But the lady asks you to persuade the Nawab to marry his cousin. After the marriage, he inherits all the property. There's no one else in line. She also asks you to bear in mind that if you can save the house from ruin, you will also profit and so will they. Everything depends on you.'

Khanum answered:

'Please convey my humblest respects to the Begum Sahib, and tell her that, God willing, her instructions will be carried out in full. I remain her life-long servant, and she can expect no problems from me. Please tell her to put her mind at rest.'

The old lady added: 'But the Begum has asked that Chabban should know nothing of this. He is a very obstinate young man. If he finds out about this conversation, he will never agree.'

Khanum nodded and told me not to breathe a word. Then she took the old lady aside and whispered something that I did not catch. She took her to the door and said: 'Please tell your mistress that she is too kind and really there was no need. We shall remain indebted to her forever.'

As soon as the lady left, Khanum summoned Bismillah and gave her strict instructions to treat the Nawab with even more attention than when he was in her pay.

One day, we were both sitting with the Nawab, doing our best to be nice to him, when Khanum appeared at the door. She politely asked if she might be allowed to enter, and bowed three times. I had never seen her act so reverentially before.

'And how is my lord's health today?'

The Nawab lowered his head: 'Praise be to God.'

'May God indeed perserve you. We always pray for your well-being. But still we are no more than unfortunate women who are obliged to ply our trade for money. God, however, has given you the honour of nobility. The reason for my coming into your august presence at this inconvenient time was merely to make a small request. My daughter, Bismillah, has had the distinction of being in your generous service for more than one year, but I have never presumed to disturb you. Indeed, it is very seldom that I have had the honour of being greeted by you. It is only out of the most pressing necessity that I have come now.'

Khanum was going on in this way, and all the time Bismillah was staring at her, wondering what on earth she was talking about. I had a very good idea. The Nawab was turning all the colours of the rainbow. He had his eyes lowered and listened without saying a word.

Khanum called Bua Husaini, who arrived with a pair of very expensive shawls.

'Bua, please show us the shawls. They are the ones that are for sale, aren't they?'

Hearing the words 'for sale,' the Nawab reacted as if the had been struck by lightning.

Bua Husaini displayed the shawls, rich with golden embroidery, the like of which are rarely seen. Khanum took them over to the Nawab.

'These were offered to me yesterday. The merchant wants two thousand rupees for them. People have already offered fifteen hundred, but he would not part with them. I think they would be worth seventeen hundred. If your excellency has any regard for my advancing years, I should be most grateful if you could buy them so that I may keep myself warm.'

The Nawab was silent. Bismillah was about to speak but Khanum stopped her:

'Wait, girl, don't interrupt our conversation. You ask for something every day. Please give me a chance.'

The Nawab maintained his silence, but Khanum persisted:

'Really, Nawab! A miser who provides an immediate response is better than a generous man who says nothing. Please say something. Your silence disturbs me. If it is not to be, so be it! I shall forget my humble desires. Now, sir! Please answer. What is my standing? A miserable woman of the market-place! I beg you not to ridicule me in front of these young girls.'

The Nawab's eyes flooded with tears:

'Khanum Sahib, These shawls are a trifle, but perhaps you are not aware of my position. Obviously, Bismillah and Umrao have not informed you of what has happened.'

'No. I have heard nothing. I hope all is well.'

Bismillah tried to speak again, but Khanum so fixed her with her eyes that she remained silent. I sat frozen like a statue. The Nawab spoke:

'I am no longer able to grant your wishes.'

'May your enemies be impotent. I am not so impertinent as to make such requests every day. Bismillah might, but how should an old wrech like me presume to make demands?' She heaved a long sigh of despair. 'Has fortune brought us to such a pass when a noble such as you refuses a mean request of one so indigent as I?'

As I looked at the Nawab, I could see that Khanum's every word was like the blow of dagger in his breast. At last he spoke:

'Khanum, you are the most worthy, but I am no longer in a position to meet anyone's request. That is the truth.'

He then went on to give brief account of his ruin. Khanum looked at him and said:

'Well, sir. If you are not able to attend to such a paltry matter, what right do you have to visit the houses of whores? You must be aware of what they call women like us. Have you not heard the expression that a prostitute is no one's wife? If we started giving charity, what would we eat? Come here if you please. The door will always be open, and I shan't bar you. But I should think you would have some consideration for your self-respect!'

With these words she left the room. The Nawab turned to Bismillah:

'It was a bad mistake. I shall not come again.'

'Stay,' said Bismillah, catching hold of his coat. 'Tell me what you have decided about those bracelets.'

'Oh, I don't know,' said the Nawab, obviously vexed. 'Now let me go. It's obviously useless staying here. When I see better days, I might think again.'

'But I shan't let you go.'

'What will you do? Get your mother to beat me with her slippers?'

Bismillah turned to me: 'Umrao, my sister. What got into the old cow today? She hasn't been into my room for years, and today she arrived like a monster from hell. But I don't care if my mother is angry or not, I won't end my affair with the Nawab. He may not have anything today, but you can't close your eyes to the fact that the old girl's made thousands out of him. He's had some bad luck, but surely we're not to close our eyes to everything like parrots? I'll never throw him out, even if she tells me to. If she gives me any more trouble, I swear to you, Umrao, that I'll run off with him. That's how I feel. I've said my piece.'

She turned to the Nawab and asked him where he was living.

'Oh, I'm staying in Tahsin Ganj with Makhdum Bakhsh. It's a pity I never appreciated just how loyal he was. I'm truly ashamed of myself.'

'You mean that Makhdum Bakhsh who was employed by your father. The one you sacked?' I asked.

'Yes that's the one. But I can't tell you how good he's been to me. Well, if it was God's will. . .'

With this the Nawab burst into tears, released himself from Bismillah and left the room. I thought I would have a word with him and rushed after him, but he vanished so quickly down the stairs, that I was unable to catch him. He looked awful, and Khanum's words had a profound effect on him. Of course, I knew that what she had said was just the first part of her scheme and the rest would be realised later, but I was very anxious. Supposing he were to go and swallow something? That would be a terrible disaster.

Early in the evening, Bismillah and I went to Tahsin Ganj in search of the Nawab. We found the house of Makhdum Bakhsh with some difficulty. The palanquin-bearers called out at the door, and we were greeted by a small girl, who told us that Makhdum Bakhsh was not at home, and the Nawab had not returned since morning. We waited for two hours, but when there was no sign of either of them, we went home disappointed.

The next morning, Makhdum Bakhsh came to enquire about the Nawab. Apparently, he had not come home the previous night. In the evening, his mother's servant, the same old woman who had visited Khanum, arrived in tears, looking very distraught. She also told us that the Nawab had disappeared without trace. Both the Begum and the old Nawab were besides themselves with worry.

The Nawab had been missing for four days, when one of his rings was discovered being sold in the Nakkhas. The man who was trying to sell it was taken to the police, and he told them that Imam Bakhsh's boy had given it to him. The boy was not found and Imam Bakhsh was arrested instead. At first, he denied all knowledge of the affair, but later, succumbing to Mirza Ali Beg's brow-beating, he confessed and told the following story:

'I sit by the river near the iron bridge tending a hookah. I also mind the clothes of those who go there to swim. About five days ago, a young noble—I would say he was around twenty,—a light skinned and very handsome young man—left his clothes with me. Everybody whose clothes I was minding returned, but he did not. I assumed he had come out of the river somewhere else. It was getting late, but I was still hoping he would return. Finally I was sure he had drowned. My first thought was that if I reported the incident, I would get into trouble, so I kept quiet, took the clothes with me, and went home. I found this ring in his pocket, and another one with something written on it. I was afraid to show them to anyone, but my boy's a bad character. He swiped this ring and sold it.'

Mirza Ali Beg went with his men to the man's house to pick

up the clothes and the ring on which there was a seal. They were returned to the old Nawab, and Imam Bakhsh was arrested.

Bismillah was shocked and, turning to me, said: 'So the Nawab's drowned himself. It's my mother who's to blame for his death.'

'I'm sorry. I feel bad about the day he was here. I even rushed to the door after him, but he was gone before I could stop him.'

'He was disturbed. I curse the old Nawab. If he had not cut him off from his property, he wouldn't have taken his life. His mother must be out of her mind.'

'It's awful! He was her only son. And now he's gone. First, his mother was a widow, and now this disaster has befallen them. Really the whole house has collapsed.'

I joined in the conversation: 'So, Nawab Chabban finally drowned himself. But tell me one thing. Did he know how to swim?'

'I don't know,' said Umrao. 'But why do you ask?'

'Only because Pir Macchli told me once that a person who can swim will never drown himself on purpose!'

7

کچھ اُن کو امتحانِ وفا سے غرض نہ تھی
اک زار و ناتواں کے ستانے سے کام تھا

She had no other cause to test my faith;
Her only aim—tormenting of the weak.

'Mirza Sahib! Have you ever fallen in love?'

'Good heavens, no! But you must have been in love with hundreds of people. Tell me about it. I've always wanted to know what it's like, but you never tell me.'

'I have followed the profession of a courtesan, and there is a saying about people like us that when we wish to pull a man into our net, we die for him. And no can die for someone more effectively than us. Heaving long sighs, weeping and beating our breasts for the slightest thing, going without food for days on end, standing on the edge of a well and threatening to jump, taking poison—these are all tricks of the trade. No man, however hard-hearted can escape from our wiles, but I can tell you truthfully that I have never really been in love with anyone, nor anyone with me.

Bismillah was unsurpassed in the amorous art. Angels, let alone men, could not escape her charms. Thousands fell in love with her, and she gave her heart to thousands. Among her truest lovers was a maulvi who had the appearance of a saint. He wasn't any old maulvi. He taught the most renowned Arabic classics. People would come from miles around to study with him, and in matters of the intellect he was unsurpassed. At the time I am speaking of, he must have been about seventy. Imagine his face bathed in heavenly light, his white beard, his shaven head, with turban, wearing a lose cloak and carrying a stick. Looking at him, who would ever have thought that he could fall in love with a frivolous little tart like Bismillah? But how he was in love with her!

'I'll tell you one incident that occurred, and please don't think I'm exaggerating. It is perfectly true. You had a friend. the pious Mir Sahib who died some time ago. You remember, he had a liaison with Dilbar Jan. He was a poet who appreciated fine verse. He also appreciated a pretty face, but pursued that hobby with the utmost discretion. There were few sophisticated courtesans in this city whom he hadn't visited.'

'Yes, I replied. 'I knew him very well. May God increase the fortunes of his family!'

'Well, he was present on this occasion. You might recall that Bismillah had a row with her mother, and had gone to stay for a few days in a house at the back of the bazaar.'

'No, I never visited that house.'

'Never mind, but I went there frequently, in the hope that I might reconcile Bismillah with Khanam. One evening she was reclining on a large bolster in the courtyard, and Mirza was sitting next to her. The maulvi was squatting with his legs tucked underneath him, looking fragile and vulnerable. He sat there telling his date-stone beads, and I can still hear him mumbling: *Ya Hafiz, ya Hafiz.* As soon as I arrived, Bismillah took hold of my hand and sat me down: 'Do you want to see something to make you laugh,' she whispered. I was surprised and asked her what she meant.

'Just keep looking,' she said, and went over the maulvi. There was a tall neem-tree in the garden, and she ordered the maulvi to climb it.

The poor maulvi's face went all colours of the rainbow, and he started to tremble. I fell on the ground laughing; Mir Sahib turned his face away. The maulvi first looked up to the sky, then at Bismillah, who repeated her command a second time, then a third time: 'Maulvi Sahib, I ordered you to climb the tree.'

Then the maulvi got up, placed his cloak on a stool and moved towards the tree. He stopped and once more turned to Bismillah. She frowned and grunted at him. The maulvi began to roll up his trousers, and slowly began his ascent of the tree. He got a little way up and then looked at Bismillah, as if he were asking if that was enough.

'More,' she cried.

He went higher and waited. She indicated that she wanted him to go higher. Finally he got to the top of the trunk. If he had gone any further, the branches were so slender that he would have plunged to his death. Bismillah was on the point of saying 'higher,' but I fell at her feet and begged her not to. Mir Sahib also pleaded with her, and at last she ordered him to come down. The poor maulvi had somehow or other got to the top, but the descent was another matter. It seemed he might fall at any moment, but eventually he got to the ground without mishap. He was bathed in sweat, out of breath, almost on the point of collapse, but he steadied himself with great difficulty. Putting on his slippers and draping his cloak over his shoulders, he came and sat with dignity on his stool and went on telling his beads. But there was something bothering him, and he started to fidget. His underclothing was swarming with red ants, and that greatly inconvenienced him.

'That's Bismillah for you!,' I said. Always up to something.'

'Up to something! She sat there as if nothing had happened. Not even a flicker of a smile on her face. Mir Sahib and I were absolutely amazed:

Do any other forms of torture in this world remain?
That infidel is only happy when inflicting pain.'

'The way you have described it is enough to make anyone laugh. But I suppose you have to imagine the scene. I can see it all. Bismillah, the maulvi with his holy face, Mir Sahib and you sitting by the neem-tree in the courtyard. But really one should not laugh at such incidents. I rather feel like weeping for the maulvi's stupidity. Bismillah was an amazing girl, but making a seventy year old man climb a tree was surely going a bit too far. The whole thing baffles me.'

'You probably would not understand. The problem is too subtle for you. Still I had to tell you.'

'Do go on. Are there even more subtleties to come?'

Yes, many. Just listen. As soon as the maulvi had gone, I asked Bismillah what had got into her. I told her that she might have been the cause of his death. 'Do you think I care if he dies? ' she retorted. 'I'm fed up with that disgusting old fool. Yesterday he gave my Dhannu such a beating, he almost smashed the poor little darling's bones.'

The fact is that Bismillah had a pet monkey called Dhannu.

How she dressed and pampered it. It had a satin pullover, an embroidered shirt, a lace wrap, silver bangles, a necklace, bells on its ankles, gold ear-rings, and was fed with honey-cakes and jalebis. When she brought it, it was a pathetic little thing, but after being so well fed for three years, it got fat. It was alright with people it recognized, but would go for strangers, baring its teeth. It was so strong that it was the impossible to release your hand from its grip.

The day before the maulvi had been ordered to climb the tree, he had arrived and taken his usual seat. Bismillah thought of a prank. She made a sign to the monkey, which went behind the maulvi's back and climbed on his shoulder. Feeling something, the maulvi turned round, and, seeing the monkey, tried to shake it off. It fell underneath the stool, or for all I know, went there on purpose, and began grimacinig at the maulvi. He threatened it with his stick, and the monkey fled in panic to Bismillah's lap. Bismillah, covering the animal with the hem of her dress, stroked and kissed it, and glowering at the maulvi, let out a stream of abuse at him. She did not forget the incident, and the next day gave him his punishment.

'Quite fitting.'

'No doubt about the appropriateness of the punishment. She made, as you might say, a real baboon of him.'

'Well, the Maulvi Sahib is in honoured company. After all, Qais picked up Laila's dog and kissed it,* while the maulvi not only had the temerity to throw the pet monkey to the ground, but even took his stick to it. That is well within the exigencies of love.'

One evening about eight o'clock I was in Bismillah's room listening to her singing. I was strumming the tanpura and Khalifa Ji was beating the tabla. At that moment, the revered maulvi entered. Bismillah addressed him rudely:

'So where do you think you've been this last week?'

The maulvi answered in his usual pompous manner: 'How shall I explain? You inflicted a blow of such enormity upon my person that it was arduous for me to recover my composure. But the desire to behold your countenance once more has led me in your direction.'

'Perhaps what you want to say is that I almost put you at death's door.'

We were shocked by what she said. The maulvi answered: 'All the signs were that you had.'

'By Allah! That would have been better.'

'But how would you have profited from my death.'

'Well, I could have gone to your memorial service every year. There I would have danced and sung, and kept your good name alive!'

After this conversation, we resumed our singing. Bismillah chose a most appropriate verse:

At death's approach we did not think of hell
We saw the charms of that fair infidel.

This verse put the maulvi into a state of ecstasy. His eyes were streaming with tears which dripped from his holy beard. In the meantime, the front door opened and a stranger entered. He was well-built, of medium height, and had an almond complexion, a round face and a black beard. He was dressed in a cream-coloured light over-garment, and his pyjamas were very narrow at the ankles; with this he wore velvet slippers, an extremely fine lace cap, and carried a face cloth of muslin, embroidered with flowers.

Bismillah, who obviously knew him, looked at him and

said: 'So at last you've taken the trouble to come! You wander around looking love-lorn, then forget all about me. And what about those pieces of red cloth you promised? Is that the reason why you haven't shown you face?'

The man looked embarrassed: 'No, madame! That is not the reason. I just didn't have time. My father was very ill, and I had to look after him.'

'Yes, I'm sure you're a very dutiful son. But what you don't say is that you're head over heels in love with Battan's girl, and all night long you keep her court. I get all the news, and you have the gall to tell me that your father was ill.'

Hearing his voice, the maulvi turned round and caught sight of the man. For a moment, their eyes met and the maulvi quickly turned his face away. I looked at the man and noticed that his face also flushed. He began to shake and then rushed to the door and flew down the stairs. Bismillah kept calling after him, but he did not return.

For a moment, Bismillah was bewildered, then with a frown exclaimed: 'Oh, let it pass!' I never saw the man again after that, but the maulvi attended as usual.

'Yes,' I interrupted. 'People of former times were always consistent in their behaviour.'

The singing continued, and Gauhar Mirza, guessing that I would be there, also came along. He and Bismillah used to flirt together; they would laugh and often exchanged playful blows. But I was never so petty as to be jealous. Gauhar Mirza took his seat between us and slid his arm around Bismillah's neck. He grinned: 'Ah! You're singing so beautifully today. I would love to. . .'

I looked at the maulvi and saw his forehead puckering. Gauhar Mirza fixed the maulvi with his eyes and looked him straight in the face. Then, tugging his ears with his fingers in a sign of repentance, moved back as if he were really afraid on him. Bismillah broke into uncontrollable laughter, Khalifa Ji smiled, and I hid my face in my shawl. The maulvi, however, looked extremely anxious, and rose up as if to leave. Bismillah rudely shouted at him: 'Sit down!' The poor old man resumed his seat. All Bismillah wanted to do was to show him how intimately she knew Gauhar Mirza. She continued her flirting and giggling for a long time, while the maulvi was getting more and more hot and bothered. At last I took pity on his helplessness, and let the cat out of the bag. Bismillah was obviously angry, but I said firmly to Gauhar Mirza: 'All right, you've had your fun. Time to go!'

When the maulvi realized that Gauhar Mirza was my man, and had nothing to do with Bismillah, he at once cheered up, and we left him grinning from ear to ear.

'I suppose the maulvi's love was. . .er. . .pure?'

'Like the driven snow.'

'Then he should not have been so upset.'

'Do you really believe that jealousy cannot exist in pure love?'

'Then it could not have been pure.'

'That's between him and his conscience. But I believe it was.'

Most of Khanum's girls were good-looking, but Khurshid was exceptional. She had a face like a fairy, a complexion the colour of wheat, and her features might have been fashioned by the creator himself. Her eyes shone like jewels and her limbs were perfectly formed, smooth arms and round wrists. Everything she wore looked as if it had been especially made for her and she displayed her graces with such innocence that one glance would capture the hearts of thousands. Whenever she entered a party, it seemed as if a candle had been lit; scores of beauties might be sitting there, but everyone's eyes would be on her. However, fortune did not favour her. But why blame fortune? She was her own worst enemy. She was not really suited to this profession. She was the daughter of a landowner from Baiswara*, and her face betrayed her noble birth. She had looks sent from heaven, but the curse of her beauty was that she wanted to be loved and return the love she received. Of course, there was no shortage of men who would do anything for her. First of all, she fell in love with Pyare Sahib, who spent thousands on her and really gave her his heart and soul. Khurshid put him to the test, and when she was sure of him, she gave him her heart and soul in return. For days on end, she refused to eat, and if one day he did not turn up or was late, she would howl her eyes out. We tried to give her advice: 'Look, Khurshid! You must not go on like this. Men are heartless creatures. All you have with him is a passing liaison, and a liaison has no foundation. He will never marry you. You will regret it.'

When Pyare Sahib realized that she was hopelessly in love with him, he started to play up. Sometimes he would sit with her for the whole day, and sometimes he would not bother to come at all. Then Khurshid would be in a terrible state. Khanam was annoyed by this, and soon her visits, wages, food and drink were all cut off.

The truth is that if she had been someone's wife, she would have got along very well. A husband who appreciated her worth would have drunk the water she washed her feet in. Bismillah could not have held a candle to her. She was proud, haughty, arrogant and selfish—God help us! You have already heard about the maulvi, and she rarely treated any other client better. The fact is that she was very proud of her mother's power which was undisputed. She thought that she was the only one in the world. Khanum had very high hopes of Khurshid, and if she had been more suited to the life of a prostitute, Khanum would have made thousands out of her. But in spite of her looks, she had no voice and was hopeless at dancing. All she possessed was a pretty face. At first, she received many engagements, but when people found out that she was not very good, they stopped asking for her. Her good looks, of course, attracted some of the best people, but when they arrived and found her sitting with a long face and obviously love-lorn, and then had to put up with her off-handedness and frigidity, they also went away. The only one she had left was Pyare Sahib. But just see the cruel trick played by fate. Pyare's father incurred the displeasure of the royal family. Their home and their lands were confiscated and they were left penniless. Even so, Khurshid's love remained steady and she began to insist that Pyare take her home with him. But whether it was out of respect for his friends, or more likely because he was afraid of his father, he refused, and Khurshid's hopes were dashed.

Khurshid was a very simple girl and people did her out of hundreds of rupees. She had a naïve trust in holy men. One day a faqir called Shah Sahib arrived, and claimed to be able to make two things out of one. Khurshid took off her bracelets and gold bangles and handed them to him. Shah Sahib asked for a mud pot, into which he put some black sesame seeds. Then he dropped in the bangles and put a lid over the pot. Covering it with a cloth and tying it with a cord, he took his leave, warning her not to open the pot until the next morning. With the blessings of his master, he said, the contents of the pot would be doubled. Next day she opened the pot and found nothing in it but the sesame seeds.

Once a jogi produced a black hooded cobra from his mouth and told Khurshid that it would come and bite her the next day. The poor girl took the best ear-rings from her ears and gave them to him. Khurshid never lost her temper with anyone, and such honest and sweet-tempered girls are rarely found in respectable families, let alone among prostitutes. I only saw her get angry once, and that was when Pyare Sahib came to her, wearing his wedding-suit. At first she sat silent; then her cheeks flushed and finally began to blaze like embers. She got up and tore his suit to shreds. After that came the tears which kept streaming down her face for two days. People tried to calm her, but she developed a fever which lasted for a couple of months. She was so ill that the doctors thought she had contracted tuberculosis. Finally, thank God, she recovered without having to have treatment. To all outward appearances, she broke completely with Pyare Sahib, and began seeing other men. But she never again fell in love with anyone else, and no one ever fell in love with her, mainly because of her cold, detached attitude. Her heart was no longer in the game.

It was the rainy season, one day in the Hindu month of Savan. By the end of the afternoon, the rain had stopped and the roofs and high walls of the Chowk here and there caught the sunlight. Patchy clouds were strewn over the sky, and the west was bathed in the red glow of sunset. The Chowk was thronged with people all dressed in white. The main reason for the crowd was that it was Friday, and everyone was off to the Aish Bagh fair. Khurshid, Amir Jan, Bismillah Jan and I were busy dressing up for the occasion. We had been given pea-green scarves, and were combing and plaiting our hair. Khanum Sahib was reclining before us on the plumped-up bolsters; Bua Husaini was sitting behind her smoking her curved pipe. Mir Sahib, facing Khanum, was urging her to get ready for the fair, but she was complaining that she did not feel well enough to go. In our hearts we were all praying that she would not go, because without her we would have a glorious time.

That day Khurshid looked wonderful. How her green muslin scarf suited her complexion; her purple embroidered pyjamas with wide flapping ankles and her tightly drawn blouse would cause havoc. On her arms and neck she wore light jewelled chains; she had a diamond stud in her nose; in her ears heavy gold rings. Their beauty was enhanced by her fine bracelets and pearl necklace. She stood in the room looking at herself in a full-length mirror. I can hardly describe her comeliness. If I had looked like her, I would have had to avert the evil eye from my own reflection, but she was gloomy because she no longer had anyone to admire her looks. She now despaired of Pyare Sahib and had a sad, sad face; and that very sadness highlighted her charm. One glance at that pretty face would be enough to grind one's heart to powder, and no other simile for the state of her heart comes to mind. It was as if a plaintive verse of a fine poet had just been heard, and the heart was savouring its bitter-sweet pleasure.

Bismillah was not so bad either. The dark complexion of her face with classic features, her aquiline nose and big eyes with dark pupils, her healthy, plumpish body and her smallish stature set off well her apparel—a brocade suit, a pea-green crepe scarf, hemmed with gold and silver thread, yellow satin-pyjamas, priceless jewels covering her form from top to toe, and a crown of flowers in her hair. She was just like a bride of the fourth day,* chatting and giggling coquetishly. When she arrived at the fair she began to pull faces and make eyes at all the men who passed by. Oh yes, I forgot to say that, decked out in all our finery, we had taken individual sedans, and had already arrived at the Aish Bagh fair.

There were such a crowd that you could hardly move. Here and there were toy-sellers, sweet-shops, trays loaded with savouries, fruit and garland vendors, *pan*-stalls, hookah-bearers - in short everything you expect to find at fair. But disregarding all this, one of my greatest pleasures came from looking at the people and their faces, which are especially telling at fairs and other spectacles. Happy, miserable, poor, rich, stupid, intelligent, scholarly, ignorant, noble, base, generous, mean—all these adjectives apply to the kind of faces you see.

Here comes a fellow dressed in a brocade coat, a purple jacket, tight leggings, a cornered hat and velvet slippers turned up at the toe; there goes another with a sandal-coloured scarf placed on his head at a rakish angle, all the while ogling the prostitutes. One gentleman has come to see the fair, but he looks miserable and has a furrowed brow; he walks around mumbling something to himself under his breath. He has probably had a row with his wife and has just remembered all the things he forgot to answer her back with. Another man leads a little boy along by the hand, mentioning the word 'mummy' in every sentence: 'Mummy will have dinner ready now: mummy's not feeling well; mummy will be asleep; mummy will be waking up now; don't be naughty or mummy will have to go to the doctor's.' One man has brought a little girl along dressed up in red; she is sitting on his shoulders with a tiny ring in her nose; her plaits have been tied with scarlet ribbons, and she has silver bangles on her wrists. He squeezes her wrists till they start to hurt, so as not to let anyone steal her bangles, because he will never be able to afford another pair.

Look! Here's a fellow with one of his best mates. They are joking and swearing at each other: 'Come on, have a *pan!*' He chucks his money at the *pan*-seller; he's obviously got plenty to spare, and he's not too worried about the loose change.

Then he shouts to the hookah-man. 'Hey, Saqi! Let's have a hookah here. Light it up for us!' He is joined by another friend. They swear at each other light-heartedly, embrace and ask how they are doing. Another *pan* is ordered. The best thing is that one is a Muslim and the other a Hindu. The vendor is about to offer *pan*, but the other rushes forward to grab it. Now he looks embarrassed: 'Sorry, mate! I clean forgot.' He takes some money out of his pocket, and orders two more *pans:* 'But no cardamoms, and go easy on the catechu.' He turns to his friend: 'Well, pass me the hookah then!' He's just about to detach the pipe when he sees the hookah-man staring at him. Here he loses both the hookah and his money.

Gauhar Mirza had laid out a cloth by the Pearl Lake, and we walked through the trees, enjoying ourselves at the fair till the small hours of the morning. When it was time to go home we each got into our carriages, only to find that Khurshid's one was empty. We searched for her but to no avail. Then we sent one of our men to Pyare's house. Pyare came immediately, assuring us that he had no idea where she was. He had not even been at the fair, because his wife was ill. We had no reason to believe that he was involved and were satisfied with his explanation. Further proof was that after his marriage he had become so devoted to his wife that he had given up visiting the Chowk, and stayed most of his nights at home. But his previous affection for Khurshid and probably his respect for Khanum had caused him to come promptly, as soon as he heard of her disappearance.

A month and a half after Khurshid had gone missing, a man who had all the appearances of being one of the city's wastrels came to my room. He was dark-skinned, muscular, and wore a shawl fastened around his waist and one on his head. He barged in without ceremony, and sat down on the edge of the carpet. He looked a bit mean to me, and perhaps his awkwardness was due to the fact that he had not had much experience of visiting courtesans. I was alone in my room at that time, and called out to Bua Husaini. When she entered, he sprang up and with great informality caught hold of her hand. Then he dragged her into a corner and whispered something that I could not hear. Bua Husaini listened to him and went straight to Khanum. Finally I was informed that he wished to pay one month's advance for me. He took out his purse and carelessly threw a handful of coins into Bua Husaini's outspread skirt, without bothering to count them.

'Wait a minute,' said Bua Husaini. 'How much is that?'

'Count it yourself.'

'I don't know how to.'

'I know how much there is. Seventy-five rupees. Might be a bit less or a bit more. That means three times twenty and fifteen, or a hundred less twenty-five.'

'A hundred less twenty-five. How many days is that for?'

'Fifteen days. I'll give you another fifteen days' worth tomorrow. Altogether that will come to one hundred and fifty.'

When I heard the deal going through, I was not very pleased. He was not the kind of client I really wanted, but what could I do about that? This was my profession after all, just becoming the property of anyone who came along. Bua Husaini took the money to Khanum, who, contrary to her custom, readily accepted it. I was surprised because she rarely treated the nobility with such kindness, and would usually make them wait for a day before giving her decision.

When the deal had been concluded, this man came at night to my room. About two in the morning I heard a knock on the door downstairs. The man sprang up at once and informed me that he was leaving, and would return the next evening. As he left, he gave me five ashrafis and three rings, one of which was gold bearing a ruby, another had a turquoise and the third was set with a diamond. He told me to keep these things and not to tell Khanum. I put them on my fingers and thought how beautiful they looked. I then locked them in my box, tucking them firmly into the corner.

He came the next evening when I was having a singing lesson. He sat again on the edge of the carpet and listened to my song. When the song finished, he gave the musicians five rupees each, whereupon the teacher and the violin-players began to flatter him. The *ustad* wondered where the shawl had been spun, but when he failed to make his meaning plain, he asked for it outright. But to no avail. 'Ustad ji,' said the man, 'if it's money you want, there is no problem. But I can't let you have the shawl. It is a gift from a friend.' The *ustad* pulled a face and fell silent.

The lesson finished and Bua Husaini came to collect the outstanding seventy-five rupees, which the man counted out for her. He gave her another five for herself, and she left us alone in the room. I asked him:

'Where did you see me first, that you have been so kind as to favour me?'

'A couple of months ago in Aish Bagh.'

'And it took you two months to find me?'

'I went away, and I'm due to leave again'

I now turned on all my whorish charm:

'You mean you'll abandon me.'

'No, I'm only going away for a little while.'

'Where is your house?'

'In Farrukhabad, but because of my work I am usually here.'

'And who gave you that shawl?'

'No one.'

'But I thought it must be from a very special friend.'

'No. I swear to you. There is no one else. Only you.'

'Well, give it to me.'

'I can't.'

I was very displeased by this, but then he produced a pearl necklace with emeralds, a pair of gold ear-rings with diamonds, and two gold rings, which he placed in front of me. I gladly picked them up and put them on, but I could still not understand why he refused to part with his shawl, which could not have been worth more than five hundred. I did not even care for it very much. My insistence was just a part of my role.

The man's name turned out to be Faiz Ali. He usually came very late in the evening or even at midnight. Then he would suddenly get up and leave. Sometimes, I would hear someone whistle from the street. That was his cue to dart out. I had only been with him for four weeks, and my box was already brimming over with jewels and necklaces of all descriptions, and I had lost count of the gold and silver coins. Without telling Khanum or Bua Husaini, I had amassed a fortune of over twelve thousand rupees.

Although I was not in love with Faiz Ali, I cannot say that I detested him, and I had no reason for doing so. First, he was not at all bad-looking, and second, he gave me all I wanted. Now if he was late, I started to look impatiently towards the door. Gauhar Mirza restricted his times to the day, and most of my night-time clients were given the impression that after dark I would be otherwise engaged. As soon as I heard a knock on the door, I would always find an excuse to dismiss the people who were sitting with me.

The search for Khurshid had been abortive and there was no trace of her. Faiz Ali had in the meantime grown very fond of me, and he expressed his affection in many ways. If I had not been attached earlier to Gauhar Mirza, I would have fallen in love with Faiz Ali. Still, I did not stint my affections, and made every effort to make him feel wanted and loved. I deceived him into thinking that my love for him was real, and he soon fell into my web. I never breathed a word to anyone about the presents he showered on me, and I also had to convey the requests of Khanum and Bua Husaini to him. He thought he had a duty to fulfil them, and seemed to have no regard for money at all. I have never seen such careless generosity either in nawabs or princes.

Among my clients was à certain Pannamal Chaudhury, a Hindu businessman, who would spend a couple of hours with me, then go. He enjoyed a small crowd, and so long as he was treated well, he never objected to the presence of others. He would pay me two hundred rupees a month, but when Faiz Ali started coming, he cut his visits down. Sometimes he might come every third day, sometimes once a fortnight. When he came now, he always looked a bit downcast, and would fall silent when anything was said to him. Finally, he explained the reason for his sadness. He told me that thieves had broken into his house and had stolen jewels worth over two hundred thousand rupees. He claimed that he was ruined. In my heart I had to smile at this, because his father, Channamal, was worth millions, and although two hundred thousand is a lot of money to most people, to him it would be peanuts. I did my best to console him.

He told me that burglaries were taking place every day in the city. Just recently the robbers, who appeared to have come from outside, had broken into Nawab Malika-e-Alam's palace, and then had burgled Lala Har Parsad. Mirza Ali Beg did not know where to turn, and had received no information from the well-known thieves of the city, who swore that it was none of their doing.

The next day I was sitting in my room, and heard a commotion in the Chowk. I went over to the window and peered through the blinds. There was a crowd in the street, all talking at the same time in great excitement:

— You've arrested them, haven't you?

— Well done Mirza! A good policeman!

— Have you recovered the goods?

— Quite a lot's unaccounted for. . .

— Have they got Mian Faizu?

— Yes, I think so.

And there was Miyan Faizu, in handcuffs, surrounded by a guard. His face, which I could not see, was covered with a scarf. All this happened before midday.

As usual, Faiz Ali came to my room late in the evening to tell me he was going away for a while. Once more he urged me not to show the things he had given me to anyone. 'By the way,' he said. 'Do you think you could come away with me for a bit?'

'You know that I am not my own mistress. Ask Khanum. If she agrees, I have no objection.'

'It's true what they say. You girls are very fickle. I lay down my life for you, and you give me such a cold reply. Very well, call Bua Husaini.'

Bua Husaini came along, and Faiz Ali asked her if I might accompany him for a while.

'Where to?,' asked Bua Husaini.

'Farrukhabad. I'm not just anyone, you know. I have property there. Actually, I'm going to be away for two months. If Khanum agrees, I can pay her two months' salary in advance now, and am prepared to let her have anything else she requires.'

'I'm not sure that Khanum will agree. But I can ask.'

Bua Husaini went off to Khanum, but I was sure that she would not be willing to release me.

Faiz Ali had so far treated me so well that if I had been free to choose, I would not have hesitated to go with him. I thought that when this man had behaved so well in my home, how much better he would treat me in his own. I was toying with the idea, when Bua Husaini returned to say that on no account would Khanum let me go.

Faiz Ali proposed to double my salary, but pleas fell on deaf ears. Finally he gave up, but when Bua Husaini left, I could see that he had tears in his eyes, I felt sorry for him.

Whenever I read romantic tales about fictitious beloveds, I used to curse them. Now I thought that if I did not join him, my own faithlessness and ingratitude would be proven. I made up my mind to accompany him. When he came to see me that night, I informed him of my decision to elope.

'Right,' he said. I'll be here the day after tomorrow at the usual time. I'll find a way to get you out before midnight. But no tricks, otherwise it will be bad for you.'

I answered him that it was my decision, and I would not go back on my word. But when he left, and I had time to reflect, I wondered whether I would keep my promise or not. All the time, remembering my love and my word, my heart told me to go; but from somewhere a voice kept saying: 'Umrao, do not leave!'

By the next morning, I had still not made up my mind. All day long I turned the matter over in my heart. In the evening, I happened to be alone, and as I fell asleep, I had still not reached a firm decision. I slept until dawn, and was only half awake, when Gauhar Mirza came and shook me. This disturbed me, and for the rest of the day I wandered around feeling dopy. I remembered that I had been asked to give a performance that day, and Bua Husaini came to ask me if I was ready. I had an awful headache, and told her that I would not be going. She kept on insisting that someone in my profession had no right to refuse; the request had been especially for me, and Khanum had already accepted the fee. I told her to refund it.

'But you know that Khanum never refunds money,' said Bua Husaini.

'Not even if someone is ill? Very well, if Khanum will not pay the money back, I'll give it out of my own purse. How much do I owe?'

'A hundred rupees.'

'Very well, I'll let you have it this evening.'

'The people are waiting outside now. Do you think they'll wait till evening?'

Bua Husaini had no idea how much I had in my box. In ashrafis alone there must have been over twelve hundred, not to mention the jewels. But I had no intention of opening it in her presence. I told her to let me rest for a while and come back in an hour. I was not feeling very well.

'What's the matter with you?'

'I think I'm running a temperature, and I have a splitting headache.'

She placed her hand on my forehead:

'Yes, that's true. You're a bit run down, but you'll have to give your performance the day after tomorrow. God willing, you'll feel better then. No point in refunding the money too soon.'

Before I could answer, she got up quickly and left. I was furious with her, and all sorts of bad thoughts went through my mind. If these people cared so little for my health and thought only of their own miserable gains, what was the point of stopping with them?'

I interrupted Umrao:

'Hadn't you ever thought like that before?'

'Never. But why do you ask?'

'I wonder whether Faiz Ali's push had anything to do with it.'

'That's clear.'

'It might be clear, but there's something more to it. Something more subtle. Could it be that before you had promised to run away, you had already decided to do so?'

'No, that was not the case. I was in two minds. But Gauhar Mirza's untimely arrival and Bua Husaini's insistence made my mind up for me. In addition when Faiz Ali came that night, and I saw his face and determination, my mind was made up.'

'No. I think that you had already made up your mind. Gauhar Mirza's pranks and Bua Husaini's insistence certainly annoyed you, but that was nothing unusual. It was always happening.'

'I agree. But who was trying to dissuade me? I tell you quite truly that when I was leaving. I still seemed to hear that voice crying: "Umrao! Don't go. Listen to me." I was only half way down the stairs, when someone seemed to grip my hand. But I did not listen.'

'Whoever was trying to stop you must have been amazingly strong. By not obeying the order, you suffered a great punishment.'

'I understand. It is that which urges you to do good, and stops you doing bad.'

'No, no, it was not that. What were you doing by staying in Khanum's house? From what you have said, it seems to me that you always considered your life as wrong and bad, even though you had no alternative. Compared to remaining in Khanum's house, running off with Faiz Ali and being obliged to him was much better. His kind treatment gave you the push to leave. Your interest in a person's looks, in which you were becoming something of an expert, made you a fair judge of men. I was very interested in the way you studied people's faces at the Aish Bagh fair. At this point, you were not totally clear about Faiz Ali's real business, but your study of his face and qualities, his gestures and his speech had convinced you that running off with him was not without its dangers. However, his deceitful words and your greed for money cast a veil over your eyes. That is a pity, because if you had been aware of human psychology, you would never have fallen into his trap.'

'Very well. If you can lend me a book on it, I'll try to read it up.'

Khanum's house in the Chowk was a very secure place. To the west was the bazaar; to the north and south were the tall houses which belonged to the courtesans. On one side the house of Biba Jan; on the other lived Husain Bandi; at the back was the house of Mir Husain. In short, it was a difficult place for thieves to penetrate. In addition, three watchmen patrolled the roofs throughout the night. Since Faiz Ali had been coming to see me, a special guard, called Makki, had been stationed at my door, because of the late hours he kept. His duty was to lock and unlock the door.

Faiz Ali arrived as promised. For a while we whispered together about our plan of escape, and could hear Makki stretching himself. This meant that he was awake. Faiz Ali called to him from the room: 'Here's a rupee for you, we didn't give you anything. You can shut the door now. We're around and there's nothing to fear.'

Makki touched his forehead and left. It was time for us to go. I put two changes of clothes into a bundle, and tucking my jewel-box under my arm, went quickly with Faiz Ali to the Akbari Gate. His bullock-cart had been waiting in the *nakkhas;* we both climbed in and moved off. A bit further, at the Hindola cross-roads, Faiz Ali's groom joined us with a horse and trap. By morning we were already at Mohan Ganj, and reserved a place in the *sarai* till midday. We took the food which the innkeeper's wife had prepared:

Lentils and vetch with no pepper and salt,
Cooked without butter and served without malt.

On the third day, we got to Rae Bareilly, where we bought some clothes more suitable for the journey. I had two new suits made and packed those I had worn from Lucknow in my bundle. Having ditched the cart, we hird another and set off for Mohan Lal Ganj, which is about twenty miles from Rae Bareilly. We arrived there well into the evening, and put up at the local *sarai.* Faiz Ali went to the bazaar to buy some provisions, and I was joined by a prostitute from the opposite room, whose name was Nasiban. She was well dressed and had some nice jewels, and although she was from the country, her accent was very good. Her idiom was typical of the villagers:

'Where do you come from then?'

'Faizabad.'

'I got a sister there, name of Pyari. You must know her.'

'Why should I?' By now she had recognized that I was a prostitute.

'Well, there aren't many lasses like us who don't know me in Faizabad.'

'It's long time since I've been there. He comes from Lucknow. So I'm usually there.'

'So you don't know anyone in Faizabad?'

'No.'

'And what are you doing here?'

'With him.'

'And where are you going?'

'To Unnao.'

'And you've come through Lucknow?'

'Yes.'

'So why did you leave the main road and come to this dump? You should have gone through Narpat Ganj.'

'He's got something to do in Rae Bareiily.'

'I only mentioned it because the road's very bad down there. It's the dacoits, you know, the highway robbers that people are afraid of. They've robbed hundreds of people at Palya. The road to Unnao goes that way. Look, there're just three of you. Two men and a woman, and you've got jewels round your neck. You wouldn't stand a chance. They can rob a whole caravan.'

'Well, it's just one's luck.'

'You've got some guts.'

We went on chatting about nothing important. I just remember one interesting thing. I asked her where she was going.

'Going scrounging.'

'I don't understand.'

'Don't know what scrounging is? What sort of whore are you?'

'My dear, I just don't know. Scrounging is a sort of begging isn't it?'

'Begging? My enemies should beg! But I suppose you're right really. Prostitutes are all beggars, whether they stay in one place or travel around.'

'Yes, I agree. But what's this scrounging you're talking about?'

'Well, once a year, we leave home and travel round the villages. We often visit the homes of the rich and the nobles, and they give us what they can. Sometimes we perform and sometimes we don't.'

'So that's what they call scrounging?'

'Yes, now you've got it.'

'And have you been to any nobles around here?'

'Yes. Not far away there's a fort belonging to Shambhu Dhyan Raja. I went to him. The Raja works for the king, controlling highway-robbers. I stayed there a few days, but I got fed up and came here. About five miles down the road, there's a village called Samariha, which belongs to the whores. My aunt lives there, and tomorrow I'm paying her a visit.'

'Then after that?'

'I'll stay for a while, and when the Raja comes back, I go for the fort again. There are quite a lot of prostitutes waiting for him.'

'Is the Raja fond of dancing performance?'

'I'll say!'

'So what happened?'

'Well, a prostitute came there from Lucknow, and since she's been around, nobody wants to know about us.'

'Do you know her name?'

'No. I've seen her face though. She's quite fair and is very good-looking.'

'Does she sing well?'

'Rubbish. She can't sing a note. She's all right at dancing though. The Raja's mad about her.'

'How long has she been there?'

'About six months.'

That night, I told Faiz Ali about the dangers on the road. He was, however, unperturbed, and assured me that he had made adequate provision.

The next day, we left Mohan Lal Ganj before dawn, and were followed by Nasiban's cart. Faiz Ali rode on horseback. It was not long before we reached Samariha, and Nasiban pointed out the village as soon as it came into view. The road was bounded by fields in which some peasant women were watering and weeding the grass. Around one of the wells a muscular-looking woman, wearing a loin-cloth, was driving her oxen, and another was carrying the water in a leather bucket. I wondered why women like this, who worked twice as hard as men, needed to be prostitutes, and quite frankly their faces fitted the kind of work they were doing. They looked like the women in Lucknow who make yoghurt or work in dairies. It was here that Nasiban took her leave.

About four miles further on, we came to a slope. The countryside was dotted with big caves, and a river-bank stretched out ahead of us. For as far as we could see, there were lines of thickly-leaved trees. By this time the sun was almost overhead, and it must have been getting on for midday. No one but us was travelling along the road, and the place was deserted. As soon as we got to the river, Faiz Ali drove his horse off at a pace, and I was left behind in the cart. Soon his horse disappeared from view, and then came into sight on the other side of the river.

Our cart plodded on, the driver steadying the reins, and the groom running behind the horse. Now I was alone with the driver, when suddenly I saw fifteen to twenty peasants running up to us. I was afraid when the men surrounded the cart. They had rifles on the shoulders and swords fitted to their waists, and were priming their matchlocks. One of the peasants ordered us to stop, and asked who was in the cart. The driver, without stopping, called out:

'A passenger from Rae Bareilly.'

'Then stop the cart.'

'Can't stop. I've got Khan Sahib's woman inside.'

'No men?'

'No. The men went on ahead. They'll be back shortly.'

'Get the woman out of the cart. She's only a bloody prostitute. She doesn't need purdah.'

One of the peasants drew back the curtain and pulled me out, while three other men came to surround me. Then I saw a cloud of dust rising from the river-bank and could hear the sound of horses' hooves. It was Faiz Ali, accompanied by fifteen other riders. The peasants at once fired a few rounds from their rifles, and two of the riders fell. Then our men unsheathed their swords, parried and three of the peasants dropped down. Another one of our riders were unseated. The peasants then fled, making for the river bank. The rider who was wounded had his arm bandaged and was put with me in the cart. We set off once more, this time with a rider-escort, two on one side, and some following. Faiz Ali turned to his companion whose name was Fazl Ali:

'I had trouble getting out of Lucknow. I'm lucky to have escaped with my life.'

'But you don't say what a good time you had!'

'No, That's true. You can say that again!'

'Say it again? I see you've brought a little present with you. Can I have a look at my new sister-in-law?'

'There's no purdah as far as you're concerned. Take a look.'

'I'll wait till we get home. I'll have a good look then.'

Soon the cart reached the river-bank, which was so steep that I had to get out and walk. We also had some difficulty in getting the cart up the bank. The wound of the man we were carrying had opened because of the jolting of the cart, and there was blood everywhere. On the other side of the river, we dressed the wound and washed the cart before I could get back in. It was now past midday and I was famished. We still trundled along, but the settlement was nowhere in sight. Finally, after covering another eight miles from the river, we came to a village, where there was a garden in which some tents were pitched. We tied up the horses and people started hurrying about preparing the food. Seeing our riders, a man came over from the camping ground and whispered something to Fazl Ali. I could see that what he had said to him made him worried. He rode over to Faiz Ali and began talking to him in a low voice. Faiz Ali answered: 'Very well, we'll see. But let's have a bite to eat first.'

'We don't have time to eat now. Let's get out of here quickly.'

'Right. But while they're pulling down the tents and bridling the horses, we'll get something to eat.'

I got out of the cart, and saw a rug spread out under a mango tree. On the rug were pots of curry and pieces of thick bread. Faiz Ali, Fazl Ali and I, with three other men, sat down to eat. The men appeared anxious, but still had time for a joke. In the meantime, our tents were loaded onto pack-ponies, and the horses were bridled. Once more our caravan took to the road.

We had travelled only a few miles when we were again surrounded by a large group of riders and men on foot. This time we were ready for them, and bullets started flying all over the place. Faiz Ali remained in the cart during the fight. I just sat there praying. My heart was in my mouth, and when I peeped out of the curtain, I saw men falling and dying on all sides. The men who had attacked us were from Raja Dhyan Singh's fort, and our side was losing. Fazl Ali and Faiz Ali seized their opportunity and took to their heels. A dozen or so of our company were arrested, and I was among them.

Soon after our arrest, the cart-driver, with considerable pleading, procured our release. The wounded passenger was thrown in the field where the corpses were lying, and taking his chance, he struggled up and took the road back to Rae Bareilly. The men were handcuffed, and we were all taken to the fort which was about ten miles away. Half-way along the road we were met by the Raja. When he saw me, he asked if I had come from Lucknow. I put my hands together and pleaded with him:

'Your Excellency! I know that I am guilty, but if you examine my situation, you will see that my guilt is not so great. A woman knows nothing of deceit. I had no idea.'

'No need to plead your innocence now. You are already found guilty. You will answer the questions when they are put to you.'

'As Your Excellency commands.'

'Where is your home? In Lucknow?'

'In the area of the Mint.'

The Raja ordered his men to fetch an ox-cart for me: 'She's a Lucknow courtesan, not like our country prostitutes who can stay up singing all night and then go straight to dance at a wedding in the morning.'

I continued my journey in the cart that was brought from the fort. The other men in handcuffs walked besides me. When we arrived, they were sent off somewhere; I was taken to the inner part of the court and given clean accommodation. Food was brought for me - cooked meat, fried bread, different kinds of sweets and pickles. It was the first time I had a square meal since I had left Lucknow. The next day I learned that the other prisoners had been sent back to Lucknow. I had been released, but the Raja would not let me depart. He summoned me sometime before noon and addressed me:

'Well, I have decided to free you. Faizu and Fazl Ali have escaped, but the other scoundrels have been sent back, and they will be sentenced. I can see that you are innocent, but I advise you not to mix with people like that in the future. If you wish, you may remain here for a few days. I have heard much of your singing.'

I remembered Nasiban telling me that the Raja had a courtesan from Lucknow in his pay. She must have mentioned me. When I asked him if that was so, he replied that I would soon find out.

She was summoned, and of course it was Khurshid. We saw each other, embraced and burst into tears. Then fearing the Raja, she tore herself away from me, and sat down quietly. The musicians were sent for and I sang a *ghazal* to celebrate my release. I can still remember some of the verses which put the Raja into a state of ecstasy:

The prisoner from the captor's snare has been released;
The bird which graced the garden fair has been released.

You leave me but your tresses hold me in their noose;
Name anyone who from your lair has been released.

My captor is not pleased I loved his chains so much;
This wretch with heart laid bare has been released.

He was too tender-hearted to endure my grief;
My cry that fled into the air has been released.

So many pains there are apart from wordly pains;
But who from life's most painful share has been released?

But why should I not envy those caught at this hour?
The joy of punishment unfair has been released.

Ada! You were released from those four walls of love;
My heart from my sweet captor's care has been released.

On hearing the last verse, the Raja asked me about the *nom-de-plume,* and when Khurshid told him that it was my own, he was overjoyed:

'If I had known that, I should never have released you.'

'Your Excellency can hear from the poem that my release has caused me sorrow, but your servant must obey the order.'

At this the Raja went into the kitchen, and left Khurshid and myself alone to talk. She began her story:

'Look, my dear sister, I am in no way to blame. Khanum and the Raja have been at loggerheads for some time. He invited me to come here several times, but Khanum refused point blank. At Aish Bagh, his men captured me and brought me here by force. But since I have been here, I have experienced nothing but kindness. I have every comfort.'

'Surely you can't like living among these miserable peasants.'

'That's true, but you know how I am. I detest having to go with a different man everyday. You know how Khanum treated me, but here I have dealings only with the Raja, and I get anything I ask for. Apart from that, I come from this part of the country, and everything is familiar.'

'So you don't want to go back to Lucknow?'

'I'm sorry, but I like it better here. Why don't you stay as well?'

'No. What I can do is another matter. I shall certainly not return to Lucknow. I'll go wherever God leads me. But I'll stay here for a bit.'

I remained at the Raja's fort for about a two weeks, and saw Khurshid everyday. But I started to get restless, and finally asked the Raja for permission to leave: 'If you let me go, I'll come again,' I said, but the Raja did not believe me.

'That's the way they make promises in Lucknow. But where will you go?'

'Kanpur.'

'You won't return to Lucknow?'

'Do you think I could show my face there again? How shameful to see Khanum again! Besides, all the others would laugh at me.'

Indeed, I had no intention of going back, and it also occurred to me that if I said I was returning, the Raja, fearing that I would disclose the whereabouts of Khurshid, would not release me. He obviously did not want any trouble concerning her. At last he seemed happy about my decision, and once more asked me to reassure him that I would not go to Lucknow.

'No,' I said, 'I have no one there. I do, however, have my talents, and I'll always find a patron. I couldn't face Khanum's prison any more. If I had wanted to stay with her, why do you think I left in the first place?'

The next day, the Raja sent me off with five ashrafis, a shawl and a ḥandkerchief. He also gave me a wooden cart. And also I begam my career as an itinerant whore. With a driver and two men to escort me, I made my way to Unnao, where I put up with the innkeeper, Salaru. I dimissed the escort, but kept the driver.

That evening, I was sitting outside my room listening to the shouts of the girls who worked at the inn: 'Travellers! This way for lodging! We provide *hookahs*, water, food and drink, and shade of the neem tree for your horses!'

Suddenly I caught sight of Faiz Ali's groom staring at me from the gate of the inn. He came over to me and said that Faiz Ali knew where I was and would be along late that evening. My heart began to thump. I thought that I had got rid of him where the fight had taken place, and now he had tracked me down to Unnao. When he arrived, he ordered me to leave the inn at once and dismiss my driver. He would provide a groom and horse, and we were to make our way to the other side of the Ganges. I had no alternative. As we were leaving, he had a word with Salaru, and helping me up onto the horse, gave the sign for departure.

It was with some difficulty that we reached the banks of the Ganges, where at last we found a boat. On the other side of the river, Faiz Ali assured me there would be no further danger, and by morning we reached Kanpur, where he put me up in the Lathi Mahal. He went out, but soon came back to tell me that he had found a home for us. The sedan was waiting outside.

We had not far to travel, and soon the sedan stopped outside a magnificient house. In the courtyard I saw two string-beds and a mat, on which an oddly shaped hookah was standing. I looked at it and felt sick. Faiz Ali announced that he was going to the bazaar to get some food. I told him to hurry up, because I did not want to be left in this strange house for too long.

For the rest of the day, there was no sign of him. Morning passed, then the afternoon, and finally the sun began to set. I had not eaten since the previous evening in Unnao. Then came that tiring journey through the night, during which I had not even had a sip of water. I was starving and it was already pitch-dark. What on earth was I to do now? Then I thought I heard someone walking around in the next portico; there were footsteps on the upper floor; someone was coming down to the stairs. It was midnight, and the moonlight, which had lit the walls around the courtyard, now disappeared, leaving me in total darkness. In panic, I pulled the blanket over my head and slept fitfully till the first light of the morning.

The sight that greeted me when I awoke was enough to make me appreciate all that I had left behind in Lucknow. Heaven knows what I had landed myself in for. How I remembered the luxury of my own place, where all I had to do was to call out and a man would come running with a hookah, *pan* and food. I waited all morning, but still no sign of Faiz Ali. If any respectable woman had found herself in this situation, she would have been dead by this time, but I had plenty of experience with other men. Let alone Kanpur, I knew little of the streets and alleys of Lucknow. All I had seen was the inn, the bazaar and the interior of this house. I got up and unbolted the door. I had not taken more than a few paces into the street when I saw a large group of mounted musketeers led by a uniformed officer. In their midst was none other than Faiz Ali being pushed before them in handcuffs. In panic, I took to my heels and fled into a narrow alley-way, where I saw a mosque. I thought that my wisest course of action would be to take refuge in the house of God. The door was open, and I stepped inside. Before me was a maulvi, a person with a dark complexion and a shaven head. He was strolling around in his loin-cloth. He probably thought that I had come to put something in the collection-box, and looked quite pleased to see me. When I went and stretched out my legs at the edge of the courtyard, he came over to ask my business.

'I am a traveller,' I replied. I thought I would rest in the house of Allah. If you have any objection, I shall leave.'

The maulvi was not very bright, but with a few well-chosen words, I soon had him under my spell. He kept on twisting his neck around, and looking up at the ceiling, stammering his approval:

'But. . .where do you. . .come from?'

'I must have come from somewhere, and now I intend to stay here.'

The maulvi looked awkward: 'Here?,' he stuttered. 'Here. . .in the. . .mosque?'

'No, no! In your little room.'

'There is no help or strength save in Allah?'

'My dear Maulvi Sahib. I can't see anyone else here but you.'

'Yes. I live by myself. That's why I asked your business.'

'Is there some sort of divine rule that says that no else can live here but you? I have no business in this mosque, but I may ask you the same question. What is your business here?'

'I teach the boys.'

'Well, shall I give you a lesson?'

'There is no help or strength save. . .'

'In Allah? Why do you keep talking about help and strength. Is the Devil after you?'

'The Devil is the enemy of mankind. You should fear him always.'

'No. You should fear God. What's the point of fearing the stupid Devil? Did you say you were a man?'

'Yes, of course I am!'

'Oh, I thought you were a *jinn.* Aren't you afraid of living in this mosque all by yourself?'

'What else do you expect? I'm used to living by myself.'

'That's why you look so panic-stricken. Have you never heard the Persian phrase: "Living alone sends you half-mad.'

'Well, I'm happy as I am. Just tell me your intention.'

'Intentions are only found in books. Now we are arguing about words.'

'What's the good?,' he said in Persian.

'Why should it not be so?,' I replied in the same language. I would have gone on teasing the maulvi, but I was too hungry to continue.

'But why did you go on teasing the poor priest,' I said.

'You should have seen him. Some people are born with the kind of face you just can't help laughing at.'

'But why make fun of him?'

'Oh, I don't know. He wasn't so peculiar really. A bit dark, startled eyes, long hair and beard, and a totally stupid expression on his face. He had shaved off his moustache, and wore his loin-cloth high up on his waist. On his head he had a chintz cap which was pulled down over his ears. He also had a strange way of speaking, by opening and closing his mouth in quick bursts. When he finished a sentence, he snorted. It looked as if he was eating something, and was afraid to leave his mouth open too long in case something fell out.'

'Was he really eating something?'

'No. Just chewing the cud.'

'There are a lot of half-baked mullahs who would answer his description. The kind of priests who are feared by the stupid and despised by the wise. I've seen many in my time.'

'He had another funny habit of twisting his neck around.'

'Yes, that follows. Perhaps he was worried that he might accidentally spit at you while he was pontificating.'

'Shall I tell you more?'

'No, that's enough. You have been up since morning. Carry on with your account.'

Well, I took a rupee from my pocket. The maulvi thought I was going to make a donation, and quickly stretched out his hand. 'Really there is no need,' he said.

I smiled: 'There is the greatest need. My belly is calling the praises of Allah!'

The maulvi was embarrassed, and tried to cover up his mistake:

'No, what I meant is that there is no need to worry. You may eat here.'

'Are the possibilities *de facto, de iure, de origine* or *de natura?'*

'Well not quite *de facto.* I've got a pupil coming soon to bring some food. You can share that.'

'Well, never mind about *de facto.* Obviously *de natura* is not in your power, but there is a pressing need for *de cibe.* So you'd better bring me something to eat from the bazaar.'

'Just be patient. The food will be here soon.'

'No. Patience is painful And *de realitate* I have heard that the holy month of Ramadhan, after its brief appearance in the world once a year, spends the rest of its time in your mosque.'

'It is true that at this particular moment there is nothing to hand, but my pupil will be coming shortly.'

'Well, supposing that does happen, I think that when the food arrives, it will not be sufficient for the exigencies of your pious appetite. My participation then amounts to *nihil.* There is an Arabic proverb which states that waiting is the harbinger of death, and a Persian saying that by the time you wait for the antidote to be brought from Iraq, the venom will have had its effect.'

'You seem to be very well versed.'

'Yes, but my simple mind perceives that you are not.'

'It might be so, but. . .'

'But my belly is rumbling, and you are annoying me with your silly arguments.'

'Very well. I'll get you something to eat.'

'And please hurry!'

The maulvi left under protest, and almost an hour and a half later came back with four pieces of doughy bread and a cup of blue-coloured soup. I was livid and glared at him, but the maulvi misunderstood. From the fold in his loin cloth he pulled out a selection of cowrie-shells and assorted coins for which he still used the old-fashioned names. 'There you are: four pice for the bread, and one pie for the curry. That's what I spent out of your rupee. Here's the change. Now count it carefully.'

Once more I glared at him, but hunger is an awful curse. I took a few quick mouthfuls and shouted at him:

'Is this the only food you can get in this one-eyed town?'

'Well, it's not quite the same as Lucknow, where Mahmud's shop serves fried rice round the clock.'

'But there must be a sweet-shop.'

'Yes, there's one just by here.'

'Then why did you have to go ten miles to get this rubbish? It's worse than dogs' food.'

'You might say that, but people eat it.'

'Yes. People like you. Stale doughy bread and blue soup!'

'It's not all that blue. Shall I get you some yoghurt?'

'No. Don't bother. I'm sorry.'

'Oh, please don't worry about the money. You can have the yoghurt on me.'

Before I could answer him, the maulvi went outside the mosque, and from a cool-water jar he brought out a pot of yoghurt that must have gone sour years ago, and placed it before me as if he was aiming a kick at Hatim's grave. Anyway, I swallowed the bread with a cup of brackish water, but thought better of the blue soup and yoghurt. I left him the little pile of cowrie-shells and small change. When I got up to wash my hands, the maulvi thought I was leaving the mosque: 'Take your money with you,' he called. 'That's all right,' I said. 'Light a lamp for me in the mosque.'

I washed my hands, and resuming my seat began to talk to the maulvi again. To be fair, he helped me a great deal when I was in Kanpur. Through him I managed to hire a room which was furnished with a comfortable tape bed. I bought a quilt, a white floor-sheet, curtains for my privacy, a selection of copper utensils and other necessary things. I engaged a servant to cook for me and another to do the housework; then I found two more to look after my daily affairs. I began to live quite comfortably. The main problem was finding musicians. Several came along, but I did not care for their style of playing. Finally I acquired a good tabla player, who turned out to be from Khalifa Ji's family. Now the room began to resound to the sound of music well into the night. When the news got round that a courtesan had arrived from Lucknow, many clients came to me, and the poetry once more began to flow. My engagement-book was completely full, and by doing one performance after another, I earned a lot of money, though I never really cared for the manners and speech of the people of Kanpur. I thought of Lucknow a great deal, but I was so happy with my newly found independence that I had no desire to return. I knew that if I did, I would have to join Khanum's house again, because there was no way I could pursue my profession there without her. Khanum had complete control over the other prostitutes, and no one would engage me separately. I would have also found it impossible to find high-class musicians, and without them no performance would have been successful. All my appointments in the circles that counted had depended on Khanum, and there was fierce competition. You can sell you name to ordinary people, but the aristocracy only frequented the established houses, and I would not have been accepted. In Kanpur, however, I was appreciated over and above my worth. There was hardly any noble family in the city which did not regard my presence at their weddings and other functions as a matter of pride. It is only when you leave Lucknow that you realize its special importance.

In Kanpur, for example, there was a poet from Lucknow, called Shariq, who had the highest reputation and a host of pupils. In Lucknow, however, he was completely unknown. One day a man came to see me, and in the course of conversation, which mainly concerned the art of poetry. He asked me if I knew Shariq. 'Who's Shariq?.' I asked. He became rather angry, and haughtily said that he was one of Shariq's best pupils:

'And I thought you said that you came from Lucknow,' he said.

'Yes, I did live there.'

'But how on earth can it be that you do not know of my respected teacher?'

'Well, I think that I know most of the best poets. Not only the masters, but I have also heard the work of their followers. Perhaps you can tell me his real name. It may be that I have not come across his *nom-de-plume.*'

'What's the point? His pen-name is known from east to west, north to south by all who appreciate verse. If you do not know, then I am sorry.'

'Then you will excuse me. But perhaps you exaggerate a

little. After all, you are his pupil and are obliged to speak highly of your master. But tell me his name. I might have heard of him.'

'Mir Hashim Ali Sahib, known as Shariq.'

'Yes, of course I have heard the name.' (For a while I had to wrack my brains to think what on earth this Mir Hashim Ali did.) 'Isn't he the one who recites elegies as well?'*

'Yes. He is unsurpassed in their recitation.'

'Right. Even better than Anis and Dabir?'*

'He's their contemporary.'

'But whose elegies does he recite?'

'Why should he recite the work of others? He recites his own compositions. He wrote one recently on the 17th of Rajab. Everyone is talking about it.'

'Can you remember it?'

'Not the beginning, but he wrote one stanza in praise of Ali's sword. Not only I, but the whole city knows it by heart.'

'Let me hear it, so that I might enjoy it as well.'

'It begins:

Jewelled words emerged from the scabbard of Holy Light. . .'

'By God's grace! That stanza is world-famous. I could give you the other five lines. They are amazing.'

'Yes, I'm happy you agree. You must have heard the elegy in Lucknow. And all this time you have been making out that you have never heard of my distinguished teacher, Shariq. At first I was surprised, but now I realize it was a joke.'

I wondered whether I should have told him that the verse had been written by Mirza Dabir, but I did not want to hurt his feelings.

'You did quite right,' I said. 'Otherwise you could have

ruined the poet's living for him. It is not only Shariq, but many self-styled poets go outside and recite other people's verse in their own name. A few days ago, a fellow stole the manuscript of a friend of mine, and went to recite it in Hyderabad, Deccan.* He fooled most people, but a few realized, and wrote to him. My friend said nothing of it, of course. People like that have given Lucknow a bad name. These days, even people from the villages who spend a few days studying there become Lakhnavis overnight. I'm not saying that just belonging to the city is a matter of special pride, but what's the point of lying?'

'True, but many use the title to sell their name. In fact that is what I did in Kanpur. In those days there was no train, and people rarely left the city. On the contrary, people went there in search of fame and fortune. Lucknow rose on the ashes of Delhi.'

'Nowadays that is the case with the Deccan. Lucknow fell and Hyderabad rose. I have never been there, but I have heard that every street is full of people from Lucknow.'

'You can always tell a person from Lucknow by the sweet way he talks.'

'Absolutely. The language has spread, but not everyone has the accent.'

8

اتفاقاتِ زمانہ سے یہ کچھ دور نہیں

یوں بھی ہوتا ہے کہ بچھڑے ہوئے مل جاتے ہیں

The chances dealt by time and tide blur near and far;
And those who separated once can meet again.

People who are separated from each other often meet again, even those who drifted apart in the distant past, whose reunion would have been undreamt of. Listen to one example of this:

I had been in Kanpur for something like six months. I had become so famous that my verses were on the lips of the people in every street and alley-way, and I always had a large crowd of clients in my room.

It was the hot season, and around two in the afternoon, I was lying alone on my bed. My cook was snoring in the kitchen, and my servant was sitting outside pulling the cord of the fan. The fragrant grass blinds had gone dry, and I was about to call for them to be sprinkled, when I heard someone downstairs enquiring whether the prostitute from Lucknow lived here. Durga Baniya, who owned the shop downstairs, pointed out the door to my apartment, and in a moment an old lady of about seventy with wrinkles on her face appeared. She was well-dressed and had a boy of about twelve with her.

I got up from my bed, pushed the *pan*-box towards her, and called out for a hookah to be brought. She then addressed me:

'My mistress has asked you to perform at her son's birthday. It will be a strictly female gathering.'

'But how does your mistress know of me?'

'Your singing is famous throughout the city, and what's more, she also comes from Lucknow.'

'You as well, I believe.'

'How do you know?'

'From the way you speak.'

'Yes, I do come from there. Tell me. How much do you charge for a performance?'

'The charge is common knowledge. Fifty rupees. But since your mistress comes from Lucknow, and has been gracious enough to ask me, I shall make no charge. When is it to be?'

'This evening, but take this rupee for your expenses. The rest will be worked out there.'

'There was really no need. But I shall take the rupee so as not to offend your mistress. Tell me where I am to go.'

'The house is quite far away. In Navaz Ganj. The boy will come to fetch you. But please make sure that there are no men in your party.'

'What about the musicians?'

'There is no bar on musicians and servants, but no one else.'

'No, no. I have no other men to bring with me. Please rest assured.'

In the meantime, the servant arrived with the hookah and

placed it before the old lady, who began to smoke it with great relish. I picked up a betel leaf and spread some catechu and lime on it, crushed a cardamom and prepared the *pan.* This I offered to her:

'Ah, where shall I find the teeth to eat a *pan?',* she sighed. I assured her that the *pan* had been prepared especially for her delicate mouth.

She was very pleased: 'Yes. These are the manners of our city.' With this she gave me a blessing and left, saying: 'Come a little early, just before the ceremony of tying the knot.'* 'Of course,' I replied. 'I know that this is not usually part of the performance, but since your mistress orders it, I shall certainly be there to sing the song of blessings.'

The Begum's house was about an hour's journey from the centre of the town. I arrived there at six o'clock. On the banks of the canal was a garden completely surrounded by a wall of cactus and other trees. The garden was set out in the English style and contained many beautiful trees, including coconut and date palms. The garden paths which cut through the green lawns were made of red brick; here and there were rockeries which were planted with various kinds of mountain shrubs; around the rockeries were clumps of panic-grass; there were artificial streams, where clear water flowed, the colour of pearls. At that time the gardeners were watering the plants with hoses, and flowers, which had begun to wither during the heat of the day, now became fresh and luxuriant.

The birthday celebrations was taking place in the villa, from which I could hear the sound of women's voices. I sang the song of blessing, and spontaneously chose something from the raga, Shyam Kalyan. For this I was sent an ashrafi and five rupees. Soon evening descended, and the moonlight playing on the ripples of the pool, produced an atmosphere of magic.

The splendid villa was situated on the edge of the garden in the middle of which was a pool. Around it were flower beds laid out with European plants. Connected with the pool was a raised platform, on which was a small pavilion with painted pillars. Water from the canal was channelled into the pool and the splashing cascades imparted an atmosphere of coolness. Everything looked wonderful; the fresh evening breeze playing among the flowers of so many bright hues created a scene which my eyes had never before witnessed. The platform was draped with a white cloth on which cushions had been arranged. We were asked to take our places on the platform which was connected to the house by a pathway with a canopy of climbing roses. Along this path came the Begum, and as she reached the screens, the platform was illuminated with a green light. I was asked to sing, and began with something from the raga, Kidara, especially appropriate for a summer evening. A maid with two green lamps came and placed them on the platform. She then instructed the musicians to go to the area designated for servants where they would given something to eat. The place where we were assembled was reserved only for women. When they had left, the Begum approached me, and standing up I greeted her politely. She led me onto the platform, sat down on her chair and asked me to sit in front of her. I expected her to ask me to sing, and looked carefully at her face:

Amazement in her look which brings about desire;
A countenance from which the eyes would never tire.

The garden and its atmosphere recalled a fairy-land, and before me sat a fairy queen. Her hair was parted in the middle and on either side her plaits curled down as far as her waist;

her complexion, almost pink, her high forehead, arched eyebrows, big eyes like the petals of roses, her long straight nose, her small mouth, thin delicate lips—all her features were so beautifully proportioned that nothing in them marred their perfection. In my life I have seen many beautiful women, but none to match her in charm and magnificence. Mentally, I began to compare her with Khurshid, but there was a world of difference. Khurshid's beauty bore all the traces of her profession; but in the Begum was every hallmark of nobility and aristocratic breeding. Compared to her, Khurshid was a little on the plump side; the Begum's limbs were well-formed and delicate. Khurshid always looked miserable; the Begum was joyful and gay, strewing roses with her light-hearted speech. When she laughed, you would be spell-bound and along with her simple formality there was a kind of petulance. Of course, all flatter the rich, but as a woman I would say that when such flattery is deserved, there can be no harm in it. Her attire enhanced her beauty: a fine yellow scarf on her shoulders, flowing onto her snake-skin bodice. In her ears she wore plain rubies, in her nose a diamond pin; her neck bore a simple gold chain, her arms bracelets decorated with gold flowers, her ankles plain golden bands. The beauty of her coutenance, the simplicity of her dress, the tastefulness of her jewels were all before my eyes which looked upon them in a state of amazement. I gazed at her untiringly, and my own face was then as you see it now, but for some reason she was also looking at me without letting her attention wander for a moment. When our eyes met, I experienced a feeling I am unable to describe. I do not know how to put it into words. Behind her a maid was standing with a fan; in front of her two others, one with a silver water-jug and the other with a *pan* box. For a long time the Begum looked at me without uttering a word: I was also unable to speak. At last she broke the silence:

'What is your name?'

I folded my hands: 'Umrao Jan.'

'Do you come from Lucknow? I mean the city itself?'

She asked the question in such a way that I found it difficult to answer, especially on this occasion. If I had said that my real home was Lucknow, then my intention would have been foiled; if I had said Faizabad, then I would have betrayed my secret. After giving the matter some thought, I said: 'Yes, I was brought up in Lucknow.' I somehow guessed the next question, and my supposition proved to be correct. At once, she asked:

'You mean that you were not born there.'

I hardly knew how to reply. I hesitated for a while, as if I had not quite understood the question. Then I decided to put her off by asking: 'Is your home also in Lucknow?'

'Yes, once it was. I have now adopted Kanpur as my home.'

'That is also my intention.'

'Why?'

This was another difficult question, and I did not know what story to tell. 'How shall I put it?', I replied. 'Perhaps it is better left unsaid. Such events have befallen me which do not bear repetition.'

'Never mind. Come and see me sometimes.'

'Certainly. I have no desire to leave. First of all there is your kind patronage, and secondly this beautiful garden. How could anyone not have the desire to see it again? For any woman who feels depressed such a scene possesses all the qualities of balm.'

'Can you truthfully say you like this jungle? Not a soul around, forsaken by God, miles away from the city! If you send a man to do a bit of shopping, he won't get back till nightfall. Call for help and the Devil wouldn't hear you. And if you have misfortune to fall ill, by the time the doctor comes, you're dead!'

'Well, madame. Everyone to his own taste, but I like it. I know that I could live here. I would desire nothing else in the world. I cannot imagine how anyone could fall ill in a place like this.'

'That's what I thought the first time I came here, but I soon realized that people used to the city cannot accustom themselves to such a place. In the town you have every comfort. Apart from anything else, since the Nawab has been in Calcutta, I'm so afraid that I cannot go to sleep. I know I have an armed guard, watchmen, servants and other men around, but I still feel scared. I shall give it a few more days, and if the Nawab does not return, I shall hire myself a house in town and live there.'

'Excuse my impertinence, but you seem to be a little upset. Please do not torment yourself. If you go to town, you will soon find out what it's like. It is so hot now that people are suffocating, and there are so many diseases around.'

As we were talking, the nanny brought the Begum's son. He was three years old, fair and pretty, and chattered away like a mynah-bird. For a while the Begum bounced him in her lap, and was about to return him to his nanny, when I asked to hold him for a while.

'Perhaps I shall not come just like that,' I said. But I shall certainly come to see this little fellow.'

The Begum smiled: 'Do as you please, but you must come. I beg of you.'

'Of course. But why should you beg me? If you speak like that, you won't be able to get rid of me.'

After our conversation, I sang until the maid came to announce that dinner was served. The Begum praised my singing, and taking my hand, led me off. She told her maid to make sure my musicians were properly fed, and then to dismiss them. There would be no second performance, and we would eat together. We followed the maid, who was holding a lamp, into the house, and as we went, the Begum whispered to me: 'I have a lot to say to you, but this is not the right occasion, and I have no time now. Come and have lunch with me the day after tomorrow. We'll say nothing more now. We'll have something to eat and listen to more of your singing.'

'But you have dismissed my musicians.'

'I don't want men around. I have a girl who plays the tabla well. She will accompany you.'

We went inside the house, which was decorated as beautifully as many of the royal appartments I had seen. Passing through several mirrored halls, we arrived in the dining-room, where a white cloth was spread on the ground. Two other women were waiting for us, a letter-writer and the other a companion. Both were good-looking and finely dressed.

On the cloth several dishes were laid out - pullao, biryani and other Indian rice preparations; various kinds of curry; kebabs, pickles, jams, sweets, yoghurt and cream—in fact, anything you could wish to eat. It was the best meal I had eaten since Lucknow. The Begum kept pushing things before me, and although I am usually careful about what I eat, her insistence made me take much more than I needed. Finally, we washed our hands, had *pan,* and then returned to the platform. Only the women of the household were present in our gathering. One of the maids took the tabla, the Begum strummed the sitar, and I was asked to sing.

It was eleven o'clock when we had finished eating, and by the time the music started it was midnight. At that late hour, the garden, which at great expense had been given the appearance of a wild mountainous terrain, took on a fearful and frightening air. The moon, whose light bathed one corner of the magnificient house, and appeared through the thick branches of the far-off trees, was on the point of setting, and darkness began to fall. This added further to the eeriness of the place. The trees seemed to grow taller as the low breeze moaned through their leaves. The cypresses seemed to sigh deeply and the silence was broken only by the water cascading into the surface of the pool. Suddenly a bird cried out, disturbed from its slumber. The calls of wild animals alarmed the birds, whose movement made the leaves rustle. A fish leapt up from the depths of the pool, frogs began to croak and a jackal howled. Apart from the handful of young women who sat on the platform, dressed in colourful attire and decked out in their fine jewellery, there was no one else present. The lights were extinguished by the gusts of the wind, and only two lamps continued to burn with a weird green flame, which was reflected on the water. Otherwise blackness covered this spell-bound land. To suit the time and the place, I chose the haunting strains of the raga Sohini, whose wailing notes enhanced the eeriness. We were all afraid to look in the direction of the garden, now overshadowed by the leafy, black trees. We fixed our eyes on each other's faces. In the silent darkness, my heart began to throb, and now I understood why the Begum so detested living in this place. Then the cry of a nearby jackal made us all start; this was followed by the barking of dogs. In a kind of numb panic we all fell silent, when suddenly, the Begum, raising herself up from her pillow, shrieked at something she had seen, and fainted in terror. We all rushed to her side.

At first, I thought she had been overcome by her strange fancies, but this was not the case. Before us stood a dozen men with masks over their faces brandishing unsheathed swords. The sound of the Begum's shrieking had aroused the servants, who came rushing to our aid. They only had sticks in their hands and were outnumbered by the robbers. Still they formed a circle around the women and stood in defiance, ready to fight or die. The other women were still unconscious; only I, with my hard heart, faced the crowd, wondering what would happen next.

The Begum's men were about to confront the intruders, but were stopped by one of the soldiers, whose name was Sarafraz. He addressed them and asked what they wanted. One of the robbers shouted: 'We don't want to kill anyone. We are not murderers. We have no bad intentions towards your women. But if you try to stop us doing what we have come for, then we shall have to see.'

I thought I recognized the voice.

Sarafraz seemed satisfied:

'That's what I wanted to know. Very well, brothers. I'll get the keys to the house and call the women who are inside. The mistress of the house is here with us. You can go into the house and take what you please, even the womens' jewellery. I do not think the master will be any poorer for that. Most of his money is in the bank. I promise there will be no tricks. You can take my word as a soldier.'

The dacoit, whose voice I thought had recognized, approached: 'Spoken like a man,' he said. 'Now get the keys.'

Suddenly our eyes met and I knew him. I was dumbfounded, and before I could get a word out, he addressed me:

'Sister-in-law! What are you doing here?'

'I've been here since your brother went to jail.'

'Where are you living?'

'In town, but one of my sisters works for the Begum. That's how I come to be here.'

'Where's your sister?'

'Here, but she fainted when you arrived. She's not like me. She's a respectable purdah-lady, who was widowed in her youth. That's why she's in the service of the nobility.'

Fazl Ali turned to his companions:

'We'll touch nothing in this house. I am not prepared to go through with the plan. You all know why we came, but I could not bring myself to steal the property of Faizu's mistress and her sister. If he heard about this, even in jail, you know what he would do.'

Hearing this the dacoits remonstrated, but they all recognized the authority of Fazl Ali, whom they dared not disobey. Still they grumbled and complained that they were hungry, and had come all this way for nothing. They were obviously in an angry mood. Meanwhile one of them went over to Fazl Ali's side and pledged his allegiance. I recognized him to be Faiz Ali's groom. I called him over and slipped him the money I had just received from the Begum.

Fazl Ali called to Sarafraz: 'All right, I'm with you. You and your men can go now.'

'Very well, I'll dismiss my men,' said Sarafraz. But you can see what a state the women are in. The Begum has fainted. You had better go now. We'll see that you are all right.'

The dacoits went; I rushed to the pool to get some water, and had great difficulty in bringing the Begum round. When she and the other women had composed themselves. I assured them that everything was well, then I told them the whole story. She was overjoyed, and I can still remember her words:

'You see, Umrao Jan, what a pleasure it is to live in this lovely garden.'

It was now three o'clock in the morning. Everyone went into the house to sleep, and I lay down on the bed that was prepared for me on the verandah. We were all so tense that no one got to sleep till daybreak. Suddenly I was rudely awakeded by a servant who had arrived with a conveyance for me. He was anxious and a little annoyed that I had stayed overnight without informing anyone. He told me to get dressed and go back with him at once. Apparently two people had arrived to see me from Lucknow. I had a good idea that the people who had come must be Bua Husaini and Gauhar Mirza. They must have got to know of my whereabouts. I was about to leave, when I was stopped by two of the Begum's maids. They asked me to call in on her before I left. I explained that I could not stop at that moment, but promised to return as soon as possible.

My guess had been correct, and when I arrived I saw Bua Husaini and Gauhar Mirza sitting there. The old lady threw her arms around me and burst into tears:

'Allah! My daughter. How could you have such a hard heart? You love no one.'

In spite of myself I felt ashamed, and found my answer only in my tears. We walked for a while, and Bua Husaini informed me that she would return to Lucknow that very day. I did my best to persuade her to stay with me, but she would not listen. She was worried because the maulvi was ill. Bua Husaini never liked leaving her home, and it was only out of love for me that she had come. I spent the rest of the day settling my affairs, paying off the rent and my servants, and ordering a carriage into which I packed my belongings, leaving to the servants all that I did not require. The next day we reached Lucknow. The same lodging, the same house, the same room and the same faces:

My travels in the wilderness of madness soothed my heart;
Then my loved-one brought me back to face the prison door.

9

دیکھیے پہونچے کہاں تک شورشِ دل کا اثر
صرصرِ وحشت کا یہ شعلہ ہے بھڑکایا ہوا

See what effect will come from this great tumult in the heart;
The flame of panic is already fanned by howling gales.

The art of the dirge* continued to be fostered at the court of Nawab Malika Kishvar untill the fall of the Avadh Sultanate, and it was at this time that I also acquired a considerable reputation among all those who performed for Prince Mirza Sikandar Hashmat, who was known as Jarnail. After he and his wife departed for Calcutta, my connections with their family were severed.

When Mirza Birjis Qadr, the last ruler of Avadh, was put on the throne, out of past respect and also because my name was known in most royal circles, I was asked to take part in the ceremony of congratulation. But darkness has descended upon the city. Every day, houses were being looted, people arrested and murdered. It was as if the trumpet of the Day Of Judgement had already sounded. Sayyid Qutb ud Din, who was among the officers of the army, and who had been appointed to the Royal Palace, was extremely kind to me. I was often asked to stay with him, and occasionally was asked to perform.

During his short-lived reign, Birjis Qadr celebrated his eleventh birthday, and the function was arranged in great style. I remember the Kashmiri singers reciting the *ghazal,* which began:

The envy of the moonlight—Birjis Qadr!
A rare pearl glowing bright—Birjis Qadr!

My own ghazal, written for the occasion began:

The hearts of thousands will be captured by your grace;
Your lovers will have blessings from your radiant face.

'Umrao Jan,' I said. That is an extraordinary verse. Do you remember any more?'

'There were eleven in all, but I swear to you that I cannot recall any more than the one I have just recited. It was a terrible time, when we went in fear of our lives. I had written the *ghazal* down on a piece of paper, and kept it in my *pan*-box until the Queen left Qaisar Bagh. But in the confusion of her departure I lost my box with almost everything I possessed.'

'Do you remember when the Queen left Qaisar Bagh?'

'No, not the exact day. It was the second or third day after the fast,* towards the end of winter. A few days before the New Year.'

'Right. It was the 16th of March. Did you leave Qaisar Bagh with the Queen?'

'I shall never forget the way her cowardly officers were

showing off, putting on airs, flattering the Begum all the way. And how they complained! The royal family were going into exile, yet one man was only concerned that he would have to walk; another worried about provisions; yet others deplored the lack of opium or that there was no hookah! When the British army arrived from Bahraich and attacked Bondi, Sayyid Qutb ud Din was killed. The Begum fled to Nepal, and I escaped with my life to Faizabad.'

'I heard that there was a lot going on in Bondi.'

'You have heard about it! I witnessed it with my own eyes. All the exiles from Lucknow gathered there. The bazaar in Bondi resembled the Chowk more than anything else.'

'Good, but I'm not very interested in that. Tell me, what happened to all the stuff that Faizu gave you?'

'Ah! Don't ask me.'

'All lost in the Mutiny?'

'If it had been, that would not have been so bad.'

'So?'

'It's a long story. The night I eloped with Faizu, I put all the money and jewels into a box, which I carefully wrapped in a cloth. Behind Khanum's house lived a man whose name was Mir. If you climb the wall of the roof of the Imambara, you can see his house. I often used to make up my bed on the wall and chat to Mir's sister. It was to her that I entrusted my box, asking her to look after it until I returned. When I came back from Faizabad, she returned the box to me, wrapped just as when I had given it to her. During the Mutiny, every house was looted. If she had told me that my jewels had also been stolen, I would have believed her. But what an honest woman! Not a penny had been taken. Those people are really the salt of the earth. If it were not for them, where would we be?'

'So how much was there?'

'Oh, I should reckon it was worth ten to fifteen thousand rupees.'

'What happened to it?'

'It went the way it came.'

'Some people say that you lost nothing in the Mutiny, and you still have everything.'

'If I did, do you think I would be living in these conditions?'

'People say you sham poverty. If not, how could you have spent all that? You don't live too badly. You have two servants; you're well-fed and well-clothed.'

'God feeds me, and I have enough to pay my way. But nothing is left of the money you are talking about.'

'But you have not told me what happened to it.'

'What can I tell you? A kind. . .'

'I understand. One of Gauhar Mirza's tricks.'

'I didn't say so. You might be wrong.'

'I am well aware of your kind-heartedness. He is doing very well, and does not even bother about you.'

'Mirza Sahib. With a prostitute, a man is here today and gone tomorrow. Why should he bother?

Those days have gone when we used to meet. . .'

'Does he come here sometimes?'

'Why should he? I often used to visit him, and I was very fond of his wife. A little while ago they had the weaning ceremony for their baby boy. He invited me.'

'I suppose you gave him something.'

'No. What do I have left to give?'

'So Gauhar Mirza took your money.'

'Mirza Sahib! Money is not everything; it just sullies your hands. I manage to make ends meet and never go hungry. It is due to the kindness of people like you that I have no problems.'

'Undoubtedly. As I have already said, you are better off than thousands of others. God even allowed you to make your pilgrimage. But that is the reward for your good nature.'

'Yes. The Lord granted me all my wishes. Now I have made up my mind that if I can go once more to Karbala, it is there that my bones will rest. You know, Mirza, I went there with the intention of never returning, but God alone knows why I just could not get Lucknow out of my mind. If I am allowed to go there again, I shall never come back.'

10

سُن چکے حال تباہی کا مری اور سُنو
اب تمھیں کچھ مری تقریر مزا دیتی ہے

You have heard of my destruction; hear some more.
From what I tell you now, your pleasure will increase.

From Bondi the Queen and Mirza Birjis Qadr took the road to Nepal; Sayyid Qutb ud Din was killed in the fighting, and with great difficulty I made my own way to Faizabad, where I put up in an inn. Later, I hired a room near Tripolia, acquired some servants and once more settled down in my profession.

After six months in Faizabad, I found that the climate and the atmosphere suited my health; I had engagements every week, and soon my fame spread throughout the town. Thousands of people queued in the street to see me, and I was gratified by their appreciation. I often thought of all the things I did in my childhood, and felt strong emotions in my breast. At the same time I remembered the fall of the Sultanate, the Mutiny and all that had befallen Birjis Qadr. Then my thoughts would turn to my parents. I wondered if they were still alive, and if so, how they were. What were they to me now? We lived in completely different worlds. The ties of blood are strong, but would any respectable person want to meet me? If I tried to see them, I would only bring them pain. I thought of them so much, but, as I did, I quickly put the idea out of my head. The memory of Lucknow haunted me, but there was no chance of returning there. Khanum would still be alive, but I could never again submit myself to her regime, and put myself back in her prison. Any idea of recovering my money seemed useless. Even if it had not been stolen, what need did I have of it? I now had plenty to live on.

One day, a middle-aged gentleman of noble bearing entered my room. I offered him *pan* and a hookah. He told me that he was from the family of Bahu Begum.* I took this opportunity to ask him about the tomb and the servants who had worked there in the past. He told me that most of them were dead, and it was no longer the same set-up, but I pressed him further:

'There used to be an elderly *jamedar* there.'

'How on earth do you know him?'

'Before the Mutiny I came to Faizabad during Muharram. I went to see the illuminations at the tomb, and he was very kind to me.'

'You mean the *jamedar* whose daughter went away?'

'How should I know?' (The story was obviously well known.)

'There were several, but the one in charge of the illuminations was that one.'

'Did he have a son?'

'Where did you see him?'

'He had a boy with him who looked just like him. I could

tell it was his son.'

'Yes. That jamedar died before the Mutiny. His son took his place.'

So as not to arouse his suspicions, I asked him a few irrelevant questions. He asked me to perform a dirge. I sang him two, and since it was getting late, he left well contented.

I was very sad to hear of the death of my father and wept all night long. The next morning, I had an uncontrollable urge to see my brother. Two days later I was asked to give a performance in some part of the town, the name of which meant nothing to me. Near the house before which I was to perform, there was a tall tamarind tree. Screens had been erected, and a large crowd had gathered, but all of them were just ordinary people. The women were waiting in the small tiled houses before and behind the screens. My first performance began at nine o'clock and continued for three hours. I looked at the place, and had the most awful feeling. This was my house! The tamarind tree was the very one under which I used to play when I was small, and when I looked at the audience, it seemed as if I had seen many of the people before. But perhaps I was mistaken. I then came from behid the screens to have a closer look. It was true. This was my old home. I had a sudden urge to rush inside, to throw myself at my mother's feet, to put my arms around her neck. But I did not have the courage, because I knew how provincial people treated prostitutes. I also had to consider my brother's position. The Nawab had already told me that people knew the story of the *Jamedar's* daughter. But from inside me a voice kept telling me that only one thin wall now separated me from my mother, —my mother for whom my heart was aching. But what was stopping me? Then I heard the voice of a woman saying:

'Excuse me. Are you the one from Lucknow? Please come this way. Someone is asking you.'

I followed her, feeling that every step I took weighed a ton. She took me to the door of the very house which I thought was my own. Behind the rush-screens a few other women were standing. They began to question me, and asked my name. At first, I wanted to say 'Amiran,' but I stopped myself just in time.

'Umrao Jan.'

'Do you come from Lucknow?'

I could no longer hold back my tears: 'No. I was born here. In this place where I am standing now.'

'You mean you were born in Bangla?'

My voice was stifled by my tears. Another woman joined in the interrogation:

'Are you a prostitute by caste?'

'No. Not by caste. It was my fate that led me to it.'

'But why are you crying? Tell us who you are.'

I broke down, and two other women came from behind the screen. One had a lamp in her hand, and shining it straight at my face, exclaimed:

'There! Didn't tell you it was her?'

The second woman cried: 'Ah! My Amiran!' and threw herself at my neck. We both burst into tears, unable to control ourselves.

After that, I told my whole story, and stayed with them all night long. I left at first light, and I shall never forget my mother's sad, longing eyes as she watched me go.

I returned to my room, and making the excuse that I was ill, refunded the money for the day's performance. The bridegroom's father, perhaps taking pity on me, only took back half the fee. For the rest of the day I stayed locked up in my room.

The next day, I was visited by a young man who must have been in his twenties. He had a darkish complexion and was dressed in a military uniform. I sent to the bazaar for a hookah and some *pan.* There was no one else in the room. The young man frowned: 'It was you who gave the performance yesterday?'

I answered him, and could see that his eyes were blazing. He lowered his glance: 'So you've brought glory on your family name!'

I now realized who he was, and replied: 'God only knows!'

'I thought you were dead, but now I can see that you are still alive.'

'It is my shame that I did not die. I pray that my death will come soon.'

'You pray well. Death is a thousand times better than the life you lead now. Why don't you take poison?'

'I should have been given this advice before.'

'If you had any shame left in you, you would never have a set foot in this town, let alone give a performance in your own home.'

'I know, but I had no idea.'

At this, the young man flew into a rage: 'But now you will!' You will!' He pulled out his knife and held it to my throat.

At that moment, my servant returned from the bazaar with the *pan* and the hookah, and raised the alarm. The young man released my arms and burst into tears himself: 'Why should I kill a woman? Why should I kill a bloody. . .'

For a short while there was confusion. I made a sign to the servant to calm down, and she stood to one side. The young man looked at me in despair: 'Very well. But get out of his town.'

''I'll go tomorrow. But let me see my mother just one last

time.'

'Get the idea out of your head. You've spread enough scandal already.'

I went on pleading: 'You see that I do not fear death. But I care for you and your children. If I remain alive, let me have news of them.'

'For God's sake, don't mention my name to anyone.'

With that he departed, and the servant began to pester me: 'Who was that?'

'Thousands visit prostitutes. What is it to you?'

The next morning, I made preparations to go to Lucknow, and having settled my affairs in Faizabad, I left in the evening.

When I arrived at Lucknow, I went straight to Khanam's house. Nothing much seemed to have changed, except that many of the old clients had left for Calcutta or other places. There was a new administration and new laws. Asaf ud Daula's Imambara now housed a fort; many houses had been demolished and new ones built in their place. Some streets had been widened and the drains had been repaired. It was not the same Lucknow at all.

I stayed in the old house for about nine months, and then got my own rooms. Khanum had changed and seemed not to care much about anything. She never mentioned the girls who had left, and did not bother about the money earned by those who had stayed behind. When I left, she hardly said a word, but I would go once or twice a week to sit with her. While I was there, I had a terrible problem with a Nawab called Mahmud Ali Khan. He began to visit me shortly after my arrival, then wanted to engage me on a permanent basis. Finally he started to put me under obligation. Obviously I could not live in Lucknow without seeing my old acquaintances, and when I sensed that the Nawab was becoming too possessive, I told him that I wanted to end our relationship. Before I knew it, the Nawab took me to court claiming that I was his wife. This proved disastrous, and I spent thousands fighting the case. When the first hearing went in the Nawab's favour, I had to go into hiding. I then engaged another lawyer and in the subsequent appeal the Nawab lost his case. He then threatened to cut off my nose and kill me. Just to protect my life, I had to hire an armed guard and travel everywhere in a closed carriage. Finally, I became so frustrated that I had a notice served on him to keep the peace from the chief magistrate, and in this way I escaped with my life. I spent six years in the courts over this affair, and it was with the utmost difficulty that I finally got rid of the Nawab.

To fight my case I managed to get hold of a solicitor named Akbar Ali Khan. He was a shady character who was the world's expert in double-dealing. There was nothing you could teach him about corruption or rigging trials, and no one could beat him in the art of twisting the courts around his little finger. He was a great help to me in my legal battle. Right or wrong, if it had not been for him, I would never have escaped the clutches of the Nawab. Although I had never married the Nawab, false witnesses could be produced in courts, and once the claim of the second party is upheld, there is nothing very much one can do about it. In support of his claim he produced two maulvis, whose foreheads were covered in corns from constant prostration in prayer. There they stood with their turbans on their heads, cloaks draped on their shoulders, rosaries in the hands and slippers on their feet. Every word they uttered was prefaced with 'By Allah!' and 'By the Holy Prophet,' and one look at their pious faces was enough to persuade the judge that they must be telling the truth. One of them acted for the plaintiff and the other for the accused, but in the subsequent altercation their testimony was invalidated. There was so much conflicting evidence that the Nawab lost the appeal, and Akbar Ali's fabricated evidence was accepted.

Akbar Ali remained a constant visitor to my house for a long time, and we formed a strong bond of friendship. He never took a penny from me; rather he spent his own money. I suppose that in some ways I fell in love with him. Personally, I think that no one is wholly bad, and there is some good to be found in everyone. You have probably heard it said about the thieves of the past that if you make a friend of them, then you will always get along very well. Without some element of goodness, life would be impossible.

After the court proceedings, I never allowed a stranger into my house in case he might have been sent along to spy on me or do me some harm. Akbar Ali used to come from the court in the morning, then turn up in the evening to say his prayers and have dinner. He always brought his own food along. I tried to tell him that there was no need for him to do this, but could never persuade him. It was at that time that I also began to say my prayers. Akbar Ali had a great passion for the Muharram rituals. In the holy months of Ramadhan and Muharram he made up for all the sins he had committed throughout the past year. Rightly or wrongly, that was his belief.

I answered this with my own opinion:

'That is matter of faith, not belief. Intelligent people have put sins into two categories: the first are those sins which only affect oneself; the second are those which affect other people. In my humble opinion, the first can be termed "minor sins," and the second (though not everyone would agree with me) are "major sins." The sins that have an adverse effect on others can be forgiven only by those who are affected by them. You have probably heard the verse of Khwaja Hafiz:

Drink wine and burn the prayer-mat; set fire to the mosque;
Go say your prayers to idols, but a man thou must not harm.

Umrao Jan! Remember that doing harm to your fellow-men is bad. You can never be forgiven for that, and if you are, I am sorry to say that God's power is useless.'

'I am a sinner to my finger-tips but even I tremble at the thought of harming my fellow-men!'

'But you must have harmed many hearts.'

'That is my profession. In the pursuit of harming hearts, I earned thousands of rupees, and lost just as many.'

'So what punishment do you expect?'

'There should not be any. In the way that I harmed hearts there was also much pleasure, and the pleasure makes up for the pain.'

'Well done!'

'Supposing someone sees me at a fair or in a performance and loses his heart to me. He knows he can't have me for nothing and that breaks his heart. Is that my fault? Then there may be someone who can afford me, but I am engaged with someone else, or perhaps I don't want him. It is my choice, and I can do nothing about it. After all no one has a monopoly on me. He might get hurt, but the pain is his own doing.'

'Yes, they deserve to be shot. But please don't count me among such people.'

'God forbid! You are one of those fortunate scoundrels who has never loved, nor have you been loved by anyone else. But on the other hand, you love everyone, and everyone loves you.'

'What are you saying? Can that ever be true?'

'I am not a student of logic, but I am sure that it can be so, when one thing has two sides to it. One kind of love is linked with intelligence, the other with stupidity.'

'For example?'

'An example of the first is the way I love you and the way you love me.'

'Very well, but allow me to know my own feelings of love; your own are revealed by your confession. But what about the second?'

'Well, the love of Qais for Laila.'*

'That's long out of date.'

'Well, like. . .Nazir. . .'

'Excuse me, I have just remembered a verse that suits the occasion. Hear it, and then you can continue your story:

My friend, you know the awful curse of love;
I took no heed of how my rival died.'

'You mean what happened in Calcutta?'

'Why look so far? Do you not find people like that in Lucknow?'

'The world is full of them.'

'Yes, I heard that you lived with Akbar Ali Khan.'

'Listen to what happened:

'When the Nawab won the first round of his case and I had to go into hiding, Akbar Ali invited me to stay in his home, which I did for several years. At that time, there were three people who were under the impression that I was living with him. First Akbar Ali himself; second his wife; and a third whose name I shall not mention.'

'Gauhar Mirza?'

'No. But have a guess. Write the name down on a piece of

paper and I shall tell you if you are right.'

'Very well, I've written it. Now tell me.'

'Myself.'

'That's exactly what I have written. Then what happened?'

He put me up in a small house which adjoined his own. Between the two houses was a window. It was really a miserable mud-hut, outside which was a thatched shed with two stoves. That served as a kitchen. He had a number of rude, impudent friends who visited him when I was there. Among them was a kind of noble called Shaikh Afzal Husain, who immediately started calling me "Sister-in-law." I got fed up with his stupid jokes, and the way he used to say: "Sister-in-law, give me a *pan.*" There is a limit to what you can stand, and from then on I used to push the box in front of him, so that he could help himself. He would pounce on it, stick his fingers in the lime and catechu, and lick them. Another man, called Vajid Ali, used to join us for dinner. I am not sure what his relationship with Akbar Ali was. All I can remember is that he used to tell disgusting jokes.

I was becoming thoroughly tired of that house, which was always full of Akbar Ali's shady legal friends, and decided to pack my bags and move out. One day it happened that Akbar Ali had gone to fight a case in Faizabad, and Afzal Husain had gone to his village. I was alone in my part of the house, and, as soon as they had gone, I bolted my door. In the meantime, Akbar Ali's wife came through the entrance to the women's apartments. I greeted her, but she just stood in front of me saying nothing. Finally in exasperation, I pointed to my bed in the courtyard and asked her to sit down.

'To what do I owe the honour of your company today?' I asked.

'If I am disturbing you, I'll go.'

'Certainly not. This is your home. You have every right to dismiss me.'

'Come off it!' It's as much your home as mine now. Or rather, it's neither mine nor yours. It belongs to him who owns it.'

'No. May God preserve the master of the house. It belongs to him as well as you.'

'You always sit here alone. I'm also a human-being, but you never come to that part of the house. I suppose he has told you not to.'

'I do not take orders from your husband. I was waiting for your permission which you have now granted me. If you wish, I shall come now.'

'Please do.'

I went with her into the main part of the house, and before my eyes there was everything you could think of: copper pots, jars, jugs, flasks, a string-bed, a mosquito-net, cushions, carpets —all scattered around in total disorder. The courtyard was littered with rubbish, and in front of the kitchen a maid was cooking the food, around which there was a swarm of buzzing flies. The ledges were stained with red spit, and the wife's bed was piled up with junk. The maid came with the pan-box, and put it down before her. The whole box was stained with lime and catechu; the very sight of it made me feel sick. In the meantime, an old woman who lived in the area entered and sat down on her huge buttocks. She pointed to me:

'Who's that? As if I didn't know already,' she added.

I interrupted her: 'Well, madame, if you know, why ask?'

'I wasn't talking to you. I was talking to my "daughter-in-law." I'm not fit to talk to the likes of you grand ladies.'

I remained silent, and the wife snapped at her:

'Shut up, you old cow! You always poison everything you

say.'

'You always hide things from me, as if I was your enemy. I was only trying to do her a favour, and she got angry with me for nothing.'

'Well, that's enough for your favours. Do you think you own this place?'

'Why should I think that. It's the newcomers who own everything here.'

At this remark, I could not help laughing and turned my head way. The wife continued:

'Why not? After all you're my co-wife.' Turning to me, she said: 'This old lady is Khan Sahib's first wife. That's right, isn't it? You are my co-wife. I came afterwards, didn't I?'

'What sort of co-wife does that make me? I don't like this kind of talk. You're always trying to insult me. But what can one expect from women like you who learn from the company of tarts and whores? I'd been here for such a long time, but his mother never said one nasty thing to me. But this young lady's so precious that she goes round insulting all the old women in the neighbourhood.'

The wife became angry: 'I've already told you, Luddan's mother, not to come to me again. Go and sit with his mother instead.'

I was getting angry, but when I saw that she was a stupid old woman, I held my peace.

'The last thing I'd do is come here again,' mumbled the old woman.

'She's asking for trouble,' said the wife. 'What's the ugly old cow talking about.'

'Am I your servant then? I never take anything from anyone. I only came to pass the time of day with you. But I won't come again.'

'Well then, don't!'

'If you're going to talk to me like that, then I *will* come. Just see if you can stop me.'

'Don't you dare, I'll give you such a beating, that you won't have a hair left on your head.'

'Go on then. Take your slippers off and hit me. You wouldn't dare, you poor little thing.'

'Get out of here!' If you don't, you'll feel my slipper.'

The old woman cackled: 'So I'm going to get a beating, am I? Go on then. Show me what a great family you come from.'

Hearing her family mentioned, the wife went red in the face, and began to tremble: 'Get out of here, I tell you!' Then turning to me, she said, 'I won't put up with it. I'll really hit the old cow!'

I tried to calm her down, but the old woman went on taunting us: 'Don't you speak to me, you scrounging whore! I'll eat you alive.'

The wife pulled her slipper from her foot: 'Take that! One! Two! Three! Now will you go?'

I pulled the slipper from the wife's hand, but she would not stop: 'You shut up as well. I'll make mincemeat out of her.'

The old lady started howling, but taking her other slipper she brought it down on her another half a dozen times. The old woman fell on the ground and began thumping her hands and screaming: 'Ow! Ow! Look, she's beating me. Now she's happy. She's getting her own back on me because she thinks I'm her co-wife. She'll murder me.'

Hearing the noise, the servant, whose name was Amiran, appeared from the kitchen, and Akbar Ali's mother, known as the elder Begum, came hurrying from the portico. Everything erupted into chaos. Seeing the Begum, the old woman once more began to thump the ground and squel: 'Look! In my old age I've been beaten with slippers.'

The Begum took pity on her: 'How was I to know that you were getting beaten. If I had, I would have come to save you. Just tell me what the problem is.'

The old woman pointed to me: That's the problem. That little tart. She's the one who started it.'

I was amazed. I did not know what to say in front of the Begum. The wife resumed: 'She is bringing her name into it again.'

'So what?' shouted the old woman. 'I only asked who she was. What's wrong with that?'

'You said you knew who she was, so what did you ask for?'

'What for? I'll tell you what for. And you see if I don't get my own back.'

The Begum was angry: 'Stop it, you old hag! Get your own back! You were probably mistaken.'

'I know I can't say anything to you, but you say what you like to me. It's your right.'

'Who are you to talk of rights? Get out of here!'

'All right. I'm going.' With that the old lady swept up her skirts, and left the house, mumbling: 'Oh, they can chuck you out. But just see. I'll be back.'

The Begum looked at the wife: 'What did you want to start an argument with with that old witch for?'

'My dear mother-in-law, I swear to you that I never said a word. She must have got out on the wrong side of the bed. But she was very rude to this poor woman.

When the Begum heard my name mentioned, she raised her eyebrows but said nothing. I had not minded the old woman's insults too much because I knew she was half mad, but the Begum's callous attitude hurt me. I got up, walked over to the window, and went back to my own apartments. I could still hear the Begum, her daughter-in-law and the cook, Amiran, talking:

'My dear girl,' said the Begum. You shouldn't have argued with the old lady. And why on earth did you stick up for that filthy prostitute?'

'Forget it. She got what she deserved for her insolence. But you might very well ask me how I come to be mixing with whore, especially with the one my husband is having an affair with. If you had been landed with her, would you make a fuss or consider it your duty to entertain her?'

The Begum turned to Amiran: 'He would never had dared to bring her, if I had anything to do with it. You can't allow anyone off the street to come into your house. His father had an affair for years with Husain Bandi. She pleaded and pleaded with me, but I never gave in. You see, my dear Amiran, I thought that if I allowed her to get her foot in the door, he would install her permanently, and no one wants to be lumbered like that. Your self-respect is in your own hands. But these days, girls give no thought to their future.'

'I agree, Begum Sahib. After all, what place do brothel-girls have in the homes of respectable people? In the past they used to say that you can invite any man into your house, but never make room for a girl from the streets.'

'Yes, but times have changed. If you let a man in now, he soon starts taking liberties with the women. Not so long ago, during the troubles, a man called Husain Khan was given shelter here. We all had to live together, but I never even let him catch a glimpse of the hem of my dress. For days on end, I hid myself away in the corner of the yard, and communicated with the servants by signs.'

'Yes, but the problem for you respectable women is just how long you can go on avoiding such people. First of all they get their fingers into the catechu pot, and while your back is turned, they've drunk a jug of water. And how far can you trust these filthy whores. They're usually full of disease. You shouldn't even let their shadow pass over you.'

'Avoid them altogether, don't let their shadow pass over you, watch out for their magic charms. But do you think she understands that. She might have given her something. You know, Mirza Muhammad's daughter-in-law was given a leech to drink by his co-wife.* She died without a child to her name.'

'I know all about that.'

'My dear! As far as this co-wife business is concerned, far better to avoid it. But even then you're not safe. That whore my husband kept tried everything. Prayers, magic charms, amulets—she pulled everything from under my pillow.'

'Then why did you let her into your house?'

'I thought she was a servant. I had no idea my husband was carrying on with her. But the day I discovered it, I chucked her out on the street.'

'But to be fair, she served you well.'

'Tried to pinch my husband! And that old woman is even worse than her. Do you know that my husband was carrying on with her as well?'

'You must be joking!'

'Would I lie? I'll have my own back.'

'But you shouldn't take your slippers to her. . . .'

'I agree. I disapproved of that myself. Beat your husband's mistress one day, and you'll be beating your mother-in-law the next.'

'Heaven preserve us, but you've got to admit that it is possible. These old women have given your daughter-in-law such a bad time of it that she was screaming her head off. I was so livid that I could have scratched their eyes out.'

I was amused by Umrao's account: 'Temper! Temper!' I said:

Keep your anger in control,
Otherwise you'll shame your soul.'

'Yes Mirza. Of course I was angry. To have such contempt for another person is inhuman.'

'I don't think you had any reason to be angry. Both the old women were right in what they said, and Luddan's mother was beaten unjustly. Whether you like it or not, she had a right. That is what I call justice. To that extent, you were not to blame. The fault lay with Ali Akbar's wife.'

'How do you make that out?'

'Well, if I had a wife like that, I would pack her straight into a carriage and send her back to her home for six months. Anyway, when Ali Akbar heard about it, what did he do?'

'He shouted his head off at the old woman, and banned her from the house, but as soon as the old Khan returned, she started coming again. He was told what had happened, and for some unknown reason he got angry with Ali Akbar's wife.'

'Was the old man in his right mind?'

'Well, he was over sixty and going a bit senile. As soon as Luddan's mother massaged his legs, he started to take her part. After all, she was his old mistress.'

'You have to admit that he showed consistency. But tell me one thing. In her youth, was the old woman, Luddan's mother, a prostitute, or was she respectable? And who was this Amiran?'

'Luddan's mother was the daughter of a miserable cotton-carder, who went wrong in her youth. Old Amiran was from a village in the Sandela district. She had a young son, who worked for Ali Akbar, and a daughter, who had been married off somewhere outside.'

'Had the old Khan had any relationship with Amiran?'

'Good heavens, no! She was a very virtuous lady. It was common knowledge that she had been widowed when she was young, and had come to work there. She would never do any wrong.'

'Well, I've heard your side of the story. Do you wish to interrogate me?'

'Are you trying to make out a case in law?'

'Yes. A very important one.

The thing is that there are three kinds of women: the virtuous, the depraved and whores! The second category can be further subdivided: one, women who sin in secret; two, those who do it openly. Among those who are virtuous you find those who would never sully their reputation; they are women who live their whole lives within four walls and put up with all kinds of affliction. Everyone is your friend when times are good, but when they are bad, you find that these poor souls will be the real friends. When their husbands are still young, and there is plenty of money, the women can get out a bit and enjoy themselves. But in times of poverty and old-age, they have no one to bother about them. They put up with hardship, and have to make the best of it. Do they not have good reason to feel proud of this? And that is why they look upon so harshly on the depraved class. God will forgive you if you are sincere in your repentance; these women will never forgive. In the case of our homely wife, no matter how beautiful, virtuous or efficient she might be, we often see that their stupid husbands get infatuated with prostitutes, even though the whore may be much less attractive than their own wife. They often abandon their wives for a while, or even permanently.

For this reason the simple wife gets an idea, or rather is certain, that the prostitute is using some supernatural force, like the charms and leeches you mentioned, that can affect her husband's mind. That is also a kind of virtue, whereby the husband is regarded as innocent, and the prostitute is given all the blame. What other proof do you require of their love?'

'That is true. But why are men so stupid?'

'The reason is that human nature craves for novelty. It becomes tired of living in one state, no matter how good that state might be, and desires constant variety. The prostitute provides a pleasure that was never before imagined. Then the man is not satisfied with just one fling, but wants to visit a different room every day.'

'But surely not all men are like that?'

'Right, but simply because the code laid down in our decent society has made such a practice reprehensible. Anyone who acts in that way will immediately incur the censure of his friends and relations, and most men do not have the courage to break the rules. But once they start mixing with the 'brother of the Devil,' and developing a taste for the forbidden fruit, they lose the fear they had in their heart. You may have noticed that when a man first visits a prostitute, he tries to keep it secret, and does not want anyone to know. Little by little, that passes, and after a while you see him picking up prostitutes in the centre of town, and even making a show of going up to their rooms. He travels around with her in an open carriage, walks around fair-grounds hand in hand with her, and even takes pride in what he is doing.'

'But in cities such behaviour is not regarded as reprehensible.'

'Especially in Delhi and Lucknow. And that is the reason why these cities have been ruined. In the country, you find far fewer depraved people who will corrupt the youth. There, prostitutes do not have so much power, because they are usually under the thumb of the nobles and the landlords, who have complete control not only over their livelihood, but even over their lives. When they meet their sons they have to be very discreet. But in the cities, there is much greater freedom, and much less control.'

'But when a man from the country goes wrong, he really does go wrong. You have already heard the story of my first client, Rashid Ali.'

'That is because they are so inexperienced. They get their first taste of fun and then don't know where to stop. People of the cities are more wordly-wise, and so their enthusiasm and addiction are more balanced.'

'I was going to ask you about your protege. What was she called?'

'You mean Abadi?'

'Yes, Abadi. She was a good-looking girl. I saw her when she was about twelve. She must have blossomed out later.'

'You have a good memory, Mirza Sahib!'

'I don't need a memory. She was such a graceful young girl. I can just imagine what she was like when she filled out.'

'In other words, you also had designs on Abadi!'

'Listen, Umrao Jan. If you catch sight of a pretty girl, always remember me, and if possible put my name down for her. Then if, God forbid! I should die, you can come and pray at my tomb.'

'What if I see a handsome man?'

'Then put your own name down, and put my name down for his sister, providing she's not classed as forbidden fruit by Islamic law!'

'Why do you have to bring Islamic law into it?'

'Why should I not involve Islamic law, especially our Islamic law from which nothing has been omitted?'

'Why don't you state your meaning plainly?. . .'

'It's often against the law, but all right according to custom.'

'That's for another occasion. But I have a principle in life, and that is to treat any good woman, whatever her religion or caste, as I would treat my own mother or sister. I deplore any action that offends against a woman's chastity, and believe that people who try to seduce such women or lead them astray should be shot. However, to enjoy the bounty offered by a bountiful lady is not, in my opinion, a sin!'

'Thank God.'

'Anyway, let's leave this nonsense, and return to what happened to Abadi Jan.'

'Mirza! If you had seen her in her prime, you would have said:

She came of age, and what a change took place!
To hell with chastity! I also changed my mind.

Her beauty was really incomparable. You would look far to find it in any other prostitute.'

'But what happened? Tell me quickly. Did she go away? I can tell by your sad tone that something must have gone wrong.'

'I lost her, and so did the world.'

'And now where is she?'

'In hospital.'

'You mean. "the flower of her youth blossomed"?'

'A nice euphemism for syphillis! By Allah! How she

blossomed. She's lost her looks and has gone as black as the bottom of that frying pan. She's got every blemish under the sun, and is now on the point of death.'

'What happened?'

'Well, she started running after the men. She went crazy and forced herself on them. I did my best for her, but to no avail. I got a teacher to educate her, but she wouldn't listen. When she matured, I gave her a room of her own, and at first a few decent clients came to her. But day and night, all you heard was shouting, brawling and fighting. I got fed up with her. She would entertain any old riff-raff, no matter how I scolded her. She had the evil eye on her from childhood. At that time, Bua Husaini's grandson, Jamman, used to play with Abadi. He was only a child, and I thought there was no harm in it. But then events took place which made me stop his visits altogether.

A man used to visit me, whose name was Chuttan. He had a nice voice, and I used to get him to sing. He was from a good family, but was a vulgar fellow himself. One evening, I caught him with Abadi in the porch. This was the sort of conversation I overheard:

"Oh Abadi! I'm so in love with you. Oh Abadi! What shall I do? I'm afraid of Umrao Jan."

"Why don't you tell me? What are you afraid of?"

I saw him put his arm round her neck.

"You torment me with your darling face."

"So what?"

He gave her a kiss. "I'm dying for you. I'm losing my life."

"That'll cost you four annas! I've seen lots of people dying, but I haven't been to their funeral yet."

"Four annas? It's my whole life I put before you."

"What do you think I need that for?"

"Is my life then so worthless?"

"Don't give me that! If you've got four annas, part with them."

"My mother hasn't had her pay yet. I'll let you have the money tomorrow."

"Right! Then you'd better stop pestering me and go."

"Just one more kiss. Please!"

He once more put his arms around her neck, and I saw Abadi going down his pocket and take out three paisas, which he happened to have on him.

"No, please don't take my money. My sister gave it to me to buy some make-up for her."

"I won't give it back."

"I'll give you four annas tomorrow."

"I want to buy a pancake now!"

"They don't cost three paisa. Just take one."

"No. I want my pancake. I've wanted it all week, but she says it'll give me belly-ache. Yesterday I bought one on the sly, and it didn't do me any harm."

'I thought: "What a little glutton! I don't know where she puts it. I had just a bite of one the other day and it gave me indigestion.'

'Perhaps you bought her during a famine!'

'Right. Her mother sold her to me for one rupee. She hadn't been fed for three days. I gave her some bread and got her for a rupee. Mirza, I feel so sorry. I asked her to stay with me, but she wouldn't.'

'Did she ever return?'

'Yes. She came probably once or twice a year. I did all I could for her, and never ill-treated her. But I haven't seen her for ages. I don't know whether she's dead or alive.'

'What was her caste?'

'Her mother was a toddy-tapper.'

'But you never finished the story. Did Chuttan give her four annas?'

'I've no idea. As soon as he had gone, I gave her a good dressing-down, and threw her out on the Chowk.

'In front of my room was another that was let out for two rupees a month to a prostitute called Husna. She was quite young and got on well with Abadi, who used to copy everything she did. Husna and her clients were alike. One of them came with half a pound of fried puris; another brought her fifty of those mangoes which sell for two annas a dozen; she would ask for a yard of *nainsukh* from one; from another she got a pair of velvet boots. When she visited fairs, she would take two ruffians with her. They would wear huge turbans and shirts with cuffs under their overcoats; sometimes they would put on dhotis and knee-breeches. They always had cudgels in their hands and chains round their necks. Husna Bibi would walk along with them wiggling her bottom. In the Stag Inn they would down a bottle of home-brewed *araq,* and emerge swaying and tottering. At same point Husna would have her arm round the waist of one, then round the neck of the other. All along the road they would swear and shout, and finally reach the fair staggering and falling about. Once there, they would smoke *charas.* The soberest one would get his hands on Husna and send the others packing. They would then go back either to his or to her room, and when the other lads returned from the fair, they would stand beneath the window shouting and throwing clods of earth at the panes. Husna would pretend not to be at home. Then a policeman would come, and break up the gathering under the illegal assembly act. Then they would all go home happy.

'That was the life-style that Abadi wanted for herself. But how could I condone it? Finally she went off with a certain Husain Ali, a servant of one of the Nawabs who used to visit me. He took her home with him, and his wife raised hell. Husain Ali was infatuated with her, and could not care less when his wife walked out on him. His main problem then was who was going to cook for him. So Abadi Bibi had to slave over the stove, something that she was not at all used to. She spent a few months in this way, and give birth to a child. God knows who the father was. Anyway two months later the child died, and Husain Ali's wife made a claim for maintenance. He was made to pay by decree one and half rupees a month. Since his salary from the Nawab was only three rupees, how could he afford it? They existed on what she could earn over and above, but that was not enough for Abadi, who had something of a sweet tooth. Finally she left Husain Ali, and went off with a boy called Mane. His mother was a Pathan brothel keeper, to whose business Abadi was a minor asset. However, one of Mane's friends, called Saadat, tricked the Pathan woman and whisked Abadi off. Mane's mother had a propensity for stealing hens, which she kept in a shed by the house. Abadi Bibi was appointed chief hen-keeper, and when Saadat went off in the morning to the factory where he worked, she used to take the hens for a walk. There she picked up with Muhammad Bakhsh, the son of Kullu, the green-grocer woman. Saadat found out about this from his mother, and gave her a hell of a beating. He had a friend called Miyan Mir, who worked for Nawab Amir Mirza. He was an expert philanderer, and took Abadi off to his own home, where she began to 'console' all his friends who usually gathered there. It was at this time when, as you put it, 'she blossoomed out.' Now she was of no used to Miyan Mir, who had her thrown into hospital, and that is where she is at present. If you wish, I'll invite her along.'

'Thank you very much.'

11

ہاتھ آئی مراد منھ مانگی
دل نے پائی مراد منھ مانگی

At last I gained my heart's desire,
From which my soul had been on fire.

It was the new moon of the month of Rajab,* and as I had nothing much to do, I thought I would visit the shrine of Hazrat Abbas.* I arrived there early in the evening and found a large crowd already assembled. I strolled around in the men's enclosure lighting candles and offering food. I listened to a man reciting an elegy, and then to a maulvi reading from the Traditions of the Prophet.* After the ritual mourning, people began to drift off to their homes. I said my last prayer and decided that it was time for me to go home as well. I got to the door, and thought that I might as well pay a visit to the women's enclosure. Because of my reputation for reciting dirges, and my former connections with the court of Malika Kishwar most of the women there would remember me. I would get talking to some of them, and would probably get an appointment. I got into my carriage, closed the curtain, and arrived at the door where the door-keeper lady helped me down from my carriage. I had not been wrong in my supposition; as soon as I entered the shrine, most of the women came up to me and began to complain about my long absence, about the dreadful events of the Mutiny and so on. We chatted for a long time, and I was about to leave, when in the courtyard I caught sight of the Begum from Kanpur. She was very smartly dressed in a heavy brocade suit, and had a retinue of half a dozen maids with her. One fussed about her pyjama-bottoms trailing on the ground; one held a fan; one carried her water jug and pan-box; one had a tray of sweets for the poor. Seeing me from afar, she ran up to me, and placed her hands on my shoulder:

'Allah! At last. How heartless you are! You disappeared without a word from Kanpur, and this is the first time I have set eyes upon you. And that too just by chance.'

'I am sorry. The morning after our night in the garden, some people came from Lucknow and took me away with them. Then came the Mutiny, and I shall not tell you what I have been through since then. I did not have your address, and you knew nothing of my whereabouts.'

'Never mind. We are both in Lucknow now.'

'In Lucknow? Let's say that we are at least in the same place.'

'That doesn't count. You must come to my home.'

'With the greatest of pleasure. But where do you live?'

'In Chaupatia. Everyone knows the Nawab.'

'I was about to ask which Nawab, when the maid interrupted: 'Everyone knows the house of Nawab Muhammad Taqi Khan.'

'I should love to come, but I hope the Nawab will not

mind.'

'Why should he? He's not that kind of man. Besides, I told him every detail of what happened in the garden that night. He tried to find you in Kanpur himself. So you must promise to come.'

'Very well, I shall come on Thursday.'

'Thursday is the night when they say spirits are abroad, and that's a whole week away. Can't you come earlier?'

'Very well. Next Monday.'

'Make it Sunday. The Nawab will be home then. On Monday I think we have an Englishman coming.'

'Fine. Sunday for certain. I can come at any time.'

'Where are you living?'

'In the Chowk. By the Sayyid Husain Khan Gate.'

'I shall send a maid for you.'

'Thank you. By the way, how is your little son?'

'Bannan? He's fine. You've just remembered him?'

'In the course of our conversation, I completely forgot.'

'He's getting on now. You'll see him when you come.'

'I shan't be able to sleep.'

'Well, this time, make sure you come.'

The maid could see that the conversation might start again, and reminded the Begum that the palanquin-bearers were getting restless.'

12

ہر چند بہت غور کیا ہم نے شب و روز
دنیا کا طلسمات سمجھ میں نہیں آتا

Though we have thought about them night and day,
The mysteries of the world we have not grasped.

I had separated from Khanum, but while she was alive, I always regarded her as my protector, and it is true that she had a great affection for me also. She had acquired such great wealth that she had no need for more, and in her old age she cared little for worldly things. She no longer bothered about how much her girls earned, but still cherished them, and never wanted them to be apart from her. I was one of her favourites. Bismillah had given her much pain, and she had developed a sort of hatred for her. Even so, she was her daughter. After the Mutiny, Khurshid Jan returned to live with Khanum; Amir Jan lived separately, but frequently paid visits.

The room that Khanum had given me so long ago always remained at my disposal. All my things were still there, and I had the key. I could come and go as I chose, and no matter where I was staying during the year, I always observed the Muharram rituals in my own room, where, until Khanum died, I kept the replica of Husain's tomb, which still bore my name.*

I had met the Begum on a Thursday. The next day, someone came to tell me that Khanum was unwell, and would like to see me. I at once called for a palanquin. I sat with Khanum for a while, and, as I was leaving, I thought I would take an embroidered gown from my room. I opened the door, and saw that it was full of cobwebs, the bed was thick with dust, the carpets were turned back, and rubbish was strewn everywhere. What a contrast from the old days, when my room used to be so neat and tidy. It would be swept four times a day, the bedding would be regularly beaten, and not a speck of dust was to be seen. Now I had no desire to sit there even for a moment, and when I looked at my bed, I had a feeling of disgust. I told the man who was with me to clean away the cobwebs with his brush. With my own hands I unrolled the rug, and we both laid it back in its place. We spread the white sheet on the floor, and taking off the matress, I gave it a beating. Then, having arranged the *pan*-box, the beauty-case and the spittoon in the way they used to be, I plumped the pillows and sat down on my bed. My man offered me a *pan,* and as I chewed it, I looked at myself in the mirror. Memories of the past came flooding back, those wonderful days when I had been young; I recalled my patrons and my clients—Gauhar Mirza's wicked playfulness, Rashid Ali's stupidity, Faizu's true love, Nawab Sultan's good looks, in short every detail of those who had sat with me in that room, which now became a magic lantern. As one picture disappeared, another came in its place. When they had all been shown, the process started over again. First they flashed before my eyes in quick succession, then there was time to pause and examine each one, to reflect upon all the events and details which had occurred with each person. My head was spinning and only a few images remained; from each picture many others emerged as the magic-lantern worked its charms around me, and I could see every episode of my life. I thought once more of Nawab Sultan, the first time I had performed before him and had looked into his eyes; the visit of his servant the next day, and his own private visits during which we would enjoy sweet conversation and verse; Khan Sahib's rude entry and Shamsher Khan's threat of suicide to save his master's honour; Sultan's absence, and then seeing him once more at the wedding party, where I sent him a note in the hands of the boy; and the happy resumption of our meetings in the house of at Navaz Ganj. The picture show went on, but as I recalled the Nawab's man bringing me his last message, it stopped. There seemed to be something missing, when I was rudely brought out of my reverie by my man's voice: 'Bibi! Watch out! There's a centipede crawling on your scarf!'

I looked in disgust, and shook the insect onto the floor. It crawled under the bed. The man lifted up the bed, and what did I see at the foot of the bed? Five golden ashrafis! The man stared in amazement: 'How on earth did they get there?'

'The centipede must have turned into gold,' I said, secretly remembering the time I had hidden them there. The man hesitated for a moment, then picked up the coins and gave them to me.

'So Khanum's house wasn't looted during the Mutiny?

'Of course it was, but do you think anyone bothered to look under my bed?'

'It's possible.'

13

کسی طرح سے ہو تسکینِ شوق کیسا رشک
ملیں گے آج ہم ان سے، رقیب سے مل کے

What balm for passion? How can jealousy arise?
Today we'll meet, but I shall meet my rival first.

The next Sunday at eight in the morning, the Begum's maid came for me with her closed carriage and palanquin-bearers. I was hardly up, and had not yet had my first hookah of the day, but she was pressing me. I told her that I would have something to eat before leaving, but she said that the Begum had given express orders that I should not have breakfast at home. I learned from her that the Nawab had already left for the village, and that he would not be back before evening. The Begum had said that we had much to talk about, and that I should hurry. I quickly washed, and taking one maid with me left my house.

The Begum was already waiting for me, and a formal breakfast was laid out: parathas, *qorma,* various types of curry, cream, rice, excellent chutney, apple jam and *halwa sohan.*

The Begum whispered: 'Do you remember how we breakfasted in Karim's house? Millet bread and vetch?'

'Hush! Don't let the others hear.'

'So what? Do you think they don't know? The Nawab's mother, God rest her soul, bought me for her son.'

'Please talk quietly. There will be gossip.'

We finished breakfast, washed our hands, had *pan* and lit our hookahs. The Begum dismissed the others.

'How did you recognize me?', I asked.

'I knew it the first time I saw you in Kanpur. I wracked my brains, wondering where I had seen you before, and then my maid, Kariman, appeared. In a flash I remembered the name of that bastard, Karim.'

'The same with me. I have a friend called Khurshid, who is a bit like you. Whenever I see her, you come to mind.'

'Well then. Listen to my story:

When we were separated, I was sold to the Nawab Sahib's mother, Umdat un Nisa Begum. You probably remember that I was about twelve at the time. The Nawab was in his sixteenth year. His father was in Kanpur, and was estranged from his wife. The Nawab's father had arranged for him to be married to his sister's daughter, who lived in Delhi, but the Begum wanted her son to marry her brother's daughter. Before that, they had not been getting on well and this was the last straw. Before the argument could develop into an all-out fight, the old Nawab was taken ill. The *hakims* urged that the marriage should be carried out as soon as possible, in case he went mad. This proved to be impossible, and it was at that time that I arrived on the scene.

The young Nawab took a liking to me, in fact he liked me so much that he refused both marriages point-blank. Within the space of a few years, the Nawab's parents, who had a great deal of property, both died. He was the only son, and inherited everything.

God bless the Nawab for making me his Begum and for providing me with the splendid style in which I now live. He loves me with as much tenderness as any man might love his truly wedded wife, and in my presence, I have never seen him look at anyone else. What he does when he is out with his friends is his own affair. He is after all a man, and I have no intention of following him around.

God has blessed me with all I could desire. I wanted children, and I have my son. My only wish is to see him grow up, be married and give me a grandson before I die. All I crave is to have my dust honoured by the Nawab. Now tell me your story.'

When I heard Ram Dai's account, I felt sorrow for my own fate, which had sold me into the house of a prostitute. I told her the tale, which you have already heard, and stayed with her for the rest of the day.

When we had finished our private chat, we asked the servants to bring us a pair of tablas, a sitar and a tanpura, and made ready for our music session. When we were alone, she was Ram Dai and I was Amiran. Before others we were the Begum Sahib and Umrao Jan, the prostitute.

We sang and played for three or four hours. The Begum managed quite well on the sitar and followed my singing with a short tune. One of her servants had a very good voice and we made her sing as well. This very enjoyable session lasted us till evening began to fall.

14

ہاں اے نگاہِ شوق مناسب ہے احتیاط
ایسا نہ ہو کہ بزم میں چرچا کرے کوئی

Oh love-lorn gaze! 'Tis better to take care,
Lest anyone should speak of what they see.

Towards evening, the Nawab's arrival was announced. Our informal concert came to an end, the instruments were put away, the purdah-ladies retired, and all was as before. I moved away from the Begum's side, and assumed a solemn air. We all looked expectantly towards the door, and the maid pulled back the curtain, calling: *Bismillah irrahman irrahim,* 'In the Name of Allah, the Compassionate and the Merciful.' The Nawab entered.

I was taken aback. It was him! It was Nawab Sultan! He was standing before me. He hesitated and looked carefully at me:

I look towards him, and I am amazed;
He sees the gaze of anguish in my eyes.

Still looking at me, he passed through the portico. The Begum greeted him:

'Look who's here. It's Umrao Jan. In Kanpur. . .'

The Nawab pretended not to know me: 'Yes, you were talking about her just a few days ago.'

He now approached the carpet, and observing the usual formalities, took his seat. The Begum joined him, sitting by his side at a slight distance.

Evening was approaching and the maid brought two lamps which shone a white light. The Begum began to prepare the *pan,* and the Nawab occasionally stole a glance at me. I did the same, but neither of us could talk. Only our eyes could express what we both felt—our complaints and misgivings, our secrets and allusions. Finally the Nawab spoke with great caution:

'Umrao Sahib! We are most grateful to you. That night in Kanpur you saved our house from being robbed.'

'Why do you embarrass me? It was a coincidence.'

'Be that as it may, it was you who saved us. There was not much in the house, but there were some important documents.'

'Yes, sir, but did you have to leave your wife alone in that jungle?'

'I had no choice. The King had confiscated my property in Lucknow, and I had to go to Calcutta to negotiate with the Governor General. Before leaving, I did not have the time to attend to everything. I only took Shamsher Khan and one other man with me.'

'But the house was so remote. It is little wonder that such a thing happened.'

'Well, we had never had any trouble before. I suppose it

was because the Mutiny was about to break out that the scoundrels became so confident. Those were dark days.'

After some general conversation, I was asked to sing. I chose the following ghazal:

Upon my death-bed I forgot the pain;
That infidel's cruel charm assailed my brain.

The love we shared the faith that we did feign,
Those you forgot, but I recalled their bane.

The night we parted soon came to an end;
Your locks still grace the couch where we have lain.

We live apart, but I remember you;
And thoughts of death come to my mind again.

The sins of love! Remember their delights;
Through them we have all Paradise to gain.

Ah healer! Give me poison from your hand;
You see, I know the remedy for pain.

I forget the other verses, but here is the last:

Who will recite a ghazal, oh. . .!
Forget the morning breeze that brings the rain.

It was the rainy season, the skies had opened, and it was pouring down. The season of mangoes. We were all assembled in my room: Bismillah Jan, Amir Jan, Bega Jan, Khurshid Jan from among the prostitutes; Nawab Babban, Nawab Chuttan, Gohar Mirza, Ashiq Husain, Tafazzul Husain, Amjad Ali, Ali Akbar Khan from among the men. Suddenly Bismillah Jan called out: 'Come on, why sit here singing? Let's put the frying pans on and cook something to celebrate the rains!'

'Why not order something from the bazaar?,' I said.

'No, we'll cook ourselves. That will be much more tasty.'

'My dear sister!' squealed Amir Jan. 'You might get fun out of clattering the pots, but I've never cooked in my life.'

Various opinions were expressed, and finally my suggestion that we should go on an outing to Bakhshi's Pool was accepted. We loaded the cooking utensils, and the tents provided by Nawab Babban onto our carts, and were off, singing as we crossed the river Gomti. The Hindi song we improvised began:

Who put up the swing in the mango grove?

How the sweet strains of that old song tugged at our heart-strings!

As we left the limits of the city, a wonderful sight greeted our eyes. The fresh green fields drenched in the rain that cascaded from the dark clouds; the boughs of the trees dripping into the swollen streams; peacocks dancing; koils calling. We talked and chattered and soon arrived at the pool, hurriedly lit our stoves and began frying puris in our clattering pans. Putting on his raincoat, Nawab Chuttan went off to hunt, and Gauhar Mirza brought back a basket of mangoes. Meanwhile the tents were put up by the servants, and bedsteads were brought from a nearby village. Everyone fell on the juicy mangoes, splashing around in the puddles, wrestling with each other, slipping and sliding, and getting thoroughly covered in the mud, which was easily washed off in the pouring rain.

Those who, like Bega Jan, were more cautious sat in the shelter of the tents. Bismillah went up behind her and rubbed mango juice all over her face, squealing in delight.

From somewhere three girl-acrobats drifted in and we asked them to sing. Their drummer was fantastic. For experts like us their performance would have been nothing special, but here in the rain all seemed absolutely in place. By early afternoon, the sky cleared and the sun came out. We had all brought a change of clothes with us, which we put on before going for a walk in the countryside.

I went off by myself to a grove where the shafts of sunlight were cutting through the thickly-leaved trees. Amid the wild flowers, birds were flying around in search of their nesting places, and as the sun shone on the lake, its surface resembled molten gold. The sky was edged with crimson, and in such an atmosphere what sensitive woman would want to return to the tents? For a long time, I wandered alone until I came to a track, along which some peasants were going. One had a plough on his shoulder, another was driving an ox, followed by a little girl leading her cows and buffaloes, and a boy with his sheep and goats. They passed by as quickly as they had appeared, and once more I was alone. For some unknown reason, I began to follow the road, thinking I would reach the pool. It was already growing dark and my shadow was lengthening in the declining sun. I went on and came to a faqir's hut, around which some people were sitting smoking their hookahs. From them I found out that I was on the road to Lucknow, and the path to the pool lay to the right. To reach it I had to leave the road and cut across rough country. Rounding a clump of trees, I spotted a person, wearing a dirty loin-cloth, a quilted jacket and a sheet wrapped around his waist. He seemed to be digging with a hoe. Our eyes met. At first I could not be sure, but when I looked carefully, I was almost certain. It was him! I could have fainted, and might well have done if I had not heard the voice of Akbar Ali Khan's servant, Salar Bakhsh, calling out for me. I was standing in front of Dilavar Khan! Resting his hoe, he glared at me, but mercifully did not seem to recognize me.

Hearing the shouts, he rushed off in the direction of the stream, and when Salar Bakhsh reached me I was trembling with fright and could not get a word out. All I could do was to point to the tree.

'What are you afraid of? There's no one there. Only a hoe. That's nothing to be afraid of. Did you think someone was digging a grave? Where did he go?'

I pointed to the stream.

'Oh, he's probably gone to have a smoke. Come on. Let's go. Nawab Chuttan's shot a lot of birds. We'd no idea where you had got to.'

Finally we arrived back at the pool and decided to stay there the whole night. When we had eaten, I told Ali Akbar the whole story.

'Are you sure it was Dilavar Khan?,' he asked. 'That fellow from Faizabad? I wish you had said earlier. We could have caught him. There's a reward out for him. What was he digging?'

'I don't know. Probably his own grave. I suppose he buried something there during the Mutiny.'

Nawab Chuttan and Bismillah were still awake in the tent, and the Nawab asked Akbar Ali what he was doing. When he explained, he asked me if I knew Dilavar Khan. Obviously I could not go through the whole story. All I said was: 'Don't worry, I know him. I remember him from Faizabad.'

'But we should do something about it,' said Akbar Ali. He

must be around here somewhere. We'll probably catch him.

With that, he asked Salar Bakhsh to bring him his pen-case, and sent a note to the nearby police-station. The police soon arrived and told us that they had already had some information from the faqir, and one of their men had been given an ashrafi dating from the imperial period. There was every chance that Dilavar Khan would be caught with his loot. The police put all their efforts into the search, and at three in the morning he was arrested at Makka Ganj with twenty-four ashrafis on him. I was called to identify him, and the next morning he was sent to the chief-magistrate in Lucknow.

'So what happened in the end?'

'Within two months he was hanged. Consigned to hell, where he belonged!'

15

نہ پوچھو نامۂ اعمال کی دل آویزی
تمام عمر کا قصہ لکھا ہوا پایا

Are you fascinated by your Book of Deeds?
There the story of your life is written bold.

Mirza Rusva! When you handed me you manuscript to check, I was so angry that I wanted to tear it to shreds. My first reaction was that when people read of my disgrace, even after my death, they would heap curses and reproaches on my head. Then I calmed down, and out of respect for your labours, I stopped my hand.

Last night, I was sleeping alone as usual when suddenly my eyes opened. All the servants were asleep downstairs, but the lamp over my pillow was still burning. For some time I tossed and turned, but I could not get back to sleep. I got up, prepared a *pan* and called for my servant to bring me a hookah. I felt like reading something, and began to turn the pages of the books I had in a case by my bed. I had read them all several times and closed them one by one. My hand then chanced upon your manuscript which I picked up with a feeling of trepidation. It is true that I had every intention of tearing it up, and was about to do so when I seemed to hear a voice saying:

'Very well, Umrao! Supposing you do rip it up and throw it away, what benefit will you derive from that? All the events of your life, which our just and powerful God has ordered the angels to record in every detail, who can erase them?'

At the sound of this voice from beyond, my very limbs began to tremble. I just stopped myself from dropping the manuscript, and the idea of destroying it passed completely from my thoughts. I wanted to replace it on the shelf, but once more I began to read it. I finished the first page, glaced at a few lines of the second, and soon became so engrossed in my own tale that I could not put it down. I have never experienced so much pleasure in reading. Most stories are simply contrived fiction, but the events you had written down were true, and had actually happened to me. I could picture them before my eyes, and the emotions they caused me I am unable to describe. If anyone had seen me that evening, they would have thought I had gone mad. Sometimes I would laugh uncontrollably; sometimes tears would fall from my eyes. You had told me to make corrections as I went through it, but I was far too carried away for that. I read until the morning, I made my ablutions, went to the lavatory, said my prayers and then fell asleep. It must have been eight in the morning when I awoke and started to read again. By evening I had finished the whole of your work.

The part I found particularly interesting was that in which you point out the difference between virtuous and depraved women. It is right that virtuous women should be proud of their behaviour, and we, who are prostitutes, should envy their pride. We should, however, be prepared to admit that chance and fortune play a large part in this. My downfall is attributable to Dilavar Khan's wickedness. If he had not abducted me and sold me to Khanum, my destiny would not have been fulfilled. Those things, which now I have no doubt were wrong, and from which I have long since repented, I could hardly have understood their true nature at that time. Nor was I aware of any law which might make me refrain from them, or persuade me that I would be punished if I did them. I believed Khanum to be my owner and master. I never did anything against her will and, if I did, I kept it well hidden in order to avoid being scolded or beaten by her. I admit that Khanum never once touched me with her cane, but the fear was always there.

I adapted to the ways of the people with whom I was brought up. At that time I never paid any attention to religious doctrine, nor I believe, would anyone else have done so in similar circumstances.

Those earthly and heavenly phenomena, for which no particular time is ordained, but which give rise to a special kind of terror which they occur - such as a sudden clap of thunder, a flash of lightning, a raging tempest, a hail-storm, an earthquake, an eclipse of the sun or the moon, famine—such things are often thought to be signs of God's wrath. But I have seen that even these can sometimes be averted by human action. On the other hand, I have witnessed many disasters that have not been put off by prayer, amulets, magic charms and spells. People consider such things to be the result of the divine will or fate decreed by heaven. I was never given instruction in the ordinances of religion, nor was the doctrine of heavenly reward explained to me. Therefore, I remained quite unaffected by such things. Undoubtedly at that time I never had any religion; I merely did what everyone else did.

I was totally without religion, and completely resigned to fate. What I could not accomplish because of indolence, or what was ruined because of faithlessness I ascribed to the whims of fortune. The books I had read in Persian taught me how to complain against the sky, and whenever my hopes were dashed, or whenever for some reason I felt depressed, willy nilly I cursed the heavens:

We are free, but free to this extent,
We blame our fate whene'er we fell constrained.

When I heard the maulvi and Bua Husaini and other elderly people talking about former times, it seemed to me that their age must have been much better than our own. For that reason I used to praise it in its absence, and for no reason reviled the age into which I was born. I never realised that they thought well of earlier times simply because everyone regards one's youth as the best, when everything in the world was so wonderful. 'When you are young, the world is young; when you are dead, the world is dead.' Young people see the elderly and adopt their ways, and this age-old misunderstanding has become a generally accepted custom.

When I reached maturity, I gave myself up to a life of pleasure and luxury. It was my profession to dance and sing and steal men's hearts. I was happy or unhappy depending on whether I was more or less successful than others in my profession. I was not as pretty as the others, but because of my talent for music and mastery of poetry, I was one of the best. I gained greater distinction than my fellows, but this proved to be injurious, because the more I excelled, the greater was my own self-esteem and pride. Whereas the other prostitutes got what they wanted through their shameless behaviour, I was left dazed and astonished. For example, it was their custom to make demands on anyone who came along; I would be ashamed to do this. I was afraid that I might be refused, and that would have hurt my pride. Nor did I easily become familiar with people. The other girls would judge their clients on what they could get out of them; I gave much more weight to a man's wit or courtesy. I thought it demeaning to ask for things. I also lacked certain other qualities found in prostitutes, and for that reason the others regarded me as aloof, neurotic or even mad! But I never paid them any attention.

Then came the time when I came to regard the mean profession of a prostitute a sin, and I washed my hands of it. I stopped entertaining just anyone who happened to come along, and restricted myself to singing or dancing. I might accept the odd engagement from a noble, but little by little, I even abandoned that.

When I repented of all those things I now considered bad, the thought occurred to me that I might settle down with some respectable gentleman. Then I remembered the saying: 'A prostitute trying to find someone to pay for her shroud.'

Mirza Sahib! Let me explain the proverb more fully. When a prostitute is getting older, and tries to settle down, experienced philanderers often say that she is 'after a shroud,' or 'she has grabbed a shroud on her death-bed.' In other words, she has saved her own money by deceiving someone into paying her funeral expenses. This proverb makes prostitutes out to be selfish, grasping and deceitful. There can be no doubt that some of us are like this. Just supposing that I have really repented and have become extremely virtuous, who apart from from God will ever know that? No one else will truly believe that I have reformed. If then I fall in love with someone, and the basis of my love is sound and well intentioned, will that person or anyone else ever trust me? So falling in love is useless. People put it about that I am wealthy, and for that reason even in my old age people still desire me, and try their best to trick me. One person even praises my beauty, even though I have heard about his judgement from other prostitutes, who are far better looking than me. Another swoons at my musical talent, though I know him to be tone-deaf. Another praises my poetry to the skies, though he could not identify a metre if he tried. Another admires my erudition and regards me superior to the most learned theologian; he even asks my advice on such simple matters as fasting and prayer, as if he would be my spiritual disciple. Another is my broken-hearted lover who does not care for my money, but only for my health and well-being. He says Allah Amen! to everything; if I sneeze, he gets a headache, and prays that his enemies might die. Another becomes my kindly adviser, and warns me of the ups and downs of the world, thinking that I am innocent like a twelve-year old girl.

But I am a wily old bird, and, as they say 'I have tasted the water of many a river-bank.' I become what people want to make me, and of course I can manipulate and hoodwink them as well. There are also a few people who are sincere, and their purpose is only to indulge their special interests, for example in poetry and song, or merely polite conversation. They want nothing else from me, nor I from them. These are the people for whom I have the greatest affection, and little by little their selflessness turns into a motive. I rely upon them, and they rely upon me. But no one like that would want to settle down with me, and that is a great pity. It is tantamount to wishing for the return of one's youth. It is true that a woman's life is as long as her youth. If only life could end at the same time as one's youth fades! But that is not so. Old age is a curse for everyone, especially for a woman, and for a prostitute, old age can be hell. If you look carefully, you will find that most of the old female beggars, whom you see dumped in the alleys of Lucknow, were once prostitutes. They were the beauties whose feet never touched the ground, and whose charms could devastate the world; they caused the deaths of hundreds of young men and brought ruin on thousands of prosperous houses. Wherever they walked, people laid down their lives for them, but now people do not give them one glance; wherever they sat, people would be overjoyed, but no one even permits them to stand in their presence. Once they would receive pearls without so much as asking, but now they are lucky to receive alms.

Most of them have brought destruction on themselves. I used to have visits from an old lady, who had at one time made for herself a great reputation among prostitutes. When she reached a certain age, she spent most of her time looking after her lovers, and in her old age moved in with a young man. But he was handsome, youthful and good-hearted, so why should he bother about her? At first his wife was angry, but when he explained what he was up to, she held her peace, and both of them began to look after her well. But when her money came to an end, and she found herself destitute, she was chucked out onto the pavement. Now she lives off scraps in back alleys.

Some stupid prostitutes procure a young girl, and bring her up, showering all their affection upon her. I also fell victim to such nonsense. But when she grows up, she soon picks up with someone, or if she stays, she gets her hands on the money and turns her mistress into a slave. Abadi would have done the same to me, but I found her out before she had the chance. Otherwise she would have ruined me.

There can, of course, be no such thing as love with prostitutes.

No sensible man would give his heart to a whore, because she knows that she can never belong to anyone or return his love. Apprentice prostitutes are always on the make, and will give nothing in return for what they receive.

Former patrons drop you as soon as you start to lose your looks. You have become used to their flattery; when there is no longer any reason for such flattery, they go away, and you end up frustrated.

At first, I used to waste my time listening to other prostitutes talking about men's faithlessness, and would automatically agree with them. But in spite of the fact that Gauhar Mirza treated me in the way that you have heard, and the Nawab, who accused me of wanting to marry him, proved troublesome, I personally never found it to be true. In matters of faith, women, and especially women of the street, are no worse than men. In fact most men are sincere in their expression of love, and most women are entirely false. The reason is to do with emotion. Men are very quick to fall under a women's spell, while women are much more cautious. Therefore men's love tends to be transitory; that of women is much longer lasting. But in a civilised society a special kind of balance is possible, on condition that both sides possess at least some understanding.

Indeed, men tend to be much more trusting, and women extremely suspicious. A man very quickly falls for a woman's charm, but a woman is much less susceptible. In my opinion this is a fault in nature. Since women are physically weaker, they have been endowed with certain qualities which make up for this deficiency. This is one important quality, which we also find in animals, where the most physically weak are also the most cunning.

Most men find women physically attractive, but I do not wholly subscribe to this view. In fact, neither men or women are attractive in themselves, and everyone has something in them which another person will find pleasing. All like a person with nice features, but the best judge of a man's beauty is a woman, and vice-versa. A beautiful woman before another woman is no more than a pretty flower without scent, but even an ugly man can be a sweetly perfumed flower for a woman, who pays less attention to his face and features. These days we see a difference in the essential nature of love. Men do not regard women in the way that women regard men. The manner in which a woman loves can to some extent be found in those men who are dependent on the favours of a rich woman, or who, though young themselves, find that an older woman has fallen in love with them.

There can be no doubt that women like younger men better than old men, but the reason for this is not only one of physical beauty. It is because the woman, being physically weak, looks first to her own safety, so that in times of necessity her man may protect her from danger. In conclusion, she can expect much more from a young man than she can from an old man. His physical charm combined with his beauty makes him irresistible. In short, all a man wishes from love is pleasure, while a woman desires both pleasure and protection from suffering.

It is often said that love should be unselfish, and this is much more important in the love felt by a woman. Therefore she tries to hide it. Someone may say that in this regard there is not much distinction to be made between men and women, and I would accept that. I would even say that these things are actually a part of the make-up of men and women, and there is no reason why they should not be aware of it. I have discovered this after the experience of a life-time, and anyone who gives attention to this will understand it. But I find that most women and uneducated men never give thought to such things. They indulge in meaningless talk, throughout the whole of their life. In my opinion, if men and therefore women knew their right place and role, they would never have any pain; many problems would be resolved and many anxieties would disappear. But the problem is that when this is explained to someone, the invariable answer is: 'What is destined to be will be.' In other words, we shall do what we wish, and please do not try to stop us! Nothing is our fault. Nothing will come of our misdeeds, since all is (may the Almighty forgive us!) ordained by God. This absurdity might have had some justification an earlier age, because some disaster was always befalling someone. I can give you an example from the royal period, when sudden changes, which radically altered people's lives, often came about.

One day, an exhausted soldier was lying asleep at the gate of the Pearl Palace. By chance, after prayers, the King passed by, and had no one else with him. For some reason, the King woke the soldier up. At first the soldier was confused, but steadying hiself, at once offered the King his sword. The King accepted the gift. The sword was so rusty that he had difficulty in pulling it out of its scabbard. The King looked at it for a moment, praised it, and returning it to his scabbard fixed it to his own belt. Then taking off his own sword, which was of foreign make, with a golden hilt and a jewel-studded belt, he presented it to the soldier. At that moment, the Grand Vizier of Avadh, Ali Naqi Khan, arrived on the scene, and before him the King praised the soldier and his sword:

'You can see, my friend, what a well turned-out young man this is, and see what a fine sword he has.'

'Your Majesty!' replied the Vizier. 'By the grace of Allah! It takes a connoisseur of fine jewels and an excellent judge of men like yourself to discern the qualities of such people and such things.'

'But see, my friend, my own sword is not so bad.'

'How could the sword of the Shadow of God be bad?'

'But his clothes are not appropriate.'

In the meantime, all the other courtiers arrived, accompanied by the mace-bearer and the royal musketeer.

'Perfectly right,' said the Vizier.

'Well, bring him a suit of my own clothes to wear.'

At this command, the people ran off and returned with trays laden with clothes. The King handed the soldier the royal suit, cut in the fashion of the period, two pearl necklaces and a pair of precious bracelets set with jewels, and had the soldier put them on.

'Now see him,' said the King.

'Indeed, he is transformed,' replied the Vizier, and his praise was echoed by all the other courtiers.

The King stayed for a while, then went off in his carriage to take the air.

The soldier went home joyfully, closely followed by jewellers, money-lenders and other brokers. They quickly made their assessment and found the clothes to be worth over fifty thousand rupees.

The soldier was a non-regular, who earned three rupees a month. The previous night at dinner, he had a row with his wife, and had left the house in a temper. After wandering around all night long, the next morning he lay down to rest by the Pearl Palace, and fell asleep. When he woke up and opened his eyes, Fortune smiled upon him, and in the twinkling of an eye, he went from rags to riches.

Such things happened in the royal period, and were made possible by the fact that the reins of government were in the hands of one person, who was subject to no rule of law. The King considered the whole wealth of the country to be his own personal property.

Under British rule, such extravagance is not possible, and the amassing of such a great fortune by one person without reason or justification is considered a kind of injustice. Under a regime in which everyone from king to beggar is under scrutiny, nothing will work unless everything can be justified. In this age, destiny has lost its force, and all is regulated and planned.

But I should tell you what happened to Nawab Chabban, an episode that was omitted from my account.

It is true that he went to drown himself, and that was his intention when he dived into the river. But life is a very precious thing, and as soon as he was under water, he panicked. He came up for air several times, and in the end found that he could not drown. At his last attempt, he had already floated as far as the Chattar Manzil, where the Heir Apparent happened to be sailing on his barge in the company of some of his attendants. Realizing that someone was in difficulties, he told his sailors to go to the rescue. It was a problem to fish him out, but they finally succeeded in pulling him ashore. When the Heir Apparent found out that he was the son of a noble, he ordered some clothes for him, and took him to his palace.

Nawab Chabban was a good-looking, refined young man who knew how to behave in society, and could fit easily into royal company. Therefore, he was given a place among the Prince's companions along with an ample salary and a handsome advance to meet his immediate requirements. Transport and servants followed. In other words, he was far better off than he had been before. Now he appeared in the Chowk seated on an elephant which was proceeded by fifty musketeers.

Bismillah and I saw him. At first we were not certain, but our suspicions were confirmed by old Makhdum Bakhsh, who was somewhere in his retinue. After that, he made peace with his uncle and married. We attended the wedding, and Khanum sent a very fine shawl and scarf. But he never again set foot in our house, nor did he have anything to do with Bismillah. Khanum tried every trick she knew, but all to no avail.

To sum up, such miracles could take place in the royal period, but you will never see them under British rule. Those days have gone when Khalil Khan used to fly his doves.* We often used to say that wealth is blind, but nowadays by some miracle it has had its eyes opened. It can recognize the one who deserves it.

In the old days, the ignorant and the illiterate, even those who could not read the first letter of the alphabet, attained high office. But can you really expect any progress where even the army was under the control of a blasted eunuch. This is not at all a laughing matter.

So destiny has had its chance, and now we are governed by plan. Now personal merit is sought, and the proceeds of merit is fame. You might be well-read and worthy, but no one even knows who you are.

I have often thought deeply about chance and plan, and have come to the conclusion that people use these terms mistakenly. If the meaning of it is that God knows all about us from the beginning of eternity, it is obvious that the infidel is the one who has no belief. But most people—may God forgive them! —attribute the results of wrong-doing to fate, and put all the blame on God. Surely they are the real infidels.

It would have been much better if I had known all this a long time ago, but I had no one to instruct me, and no experience to find it out for myself. The little that our maulvi taught me helped a great deal, but at that time I did not appreciate it. All I cared about was my own bodily comfort and ease. As well as that, my clients took up all of my time, and only when they started coming one by one did I have a moment to spare. That was when I began to get interested in reading, because I had little else to do. Truly without that interest, I would not have remained alive, and would have gone on mourning my youth or regretting losing my clients without cease.

One day I was putting my books out in the sun to air, when I came across a copy of the *Gulistan,** which I had read with my maulvi, and I began to turn over the pages. I used to hate it, because I was introduced to it too early, and I found the text difficult. But now those difficulties had disappeared, and I began to read it with the greatest pleasure. Then on someone's recommendation, I borrowed a copy of an old Persian work, the *Akhlaq-e Nasiri.** I found it very hard to understand the meaning, because it is full of Arabic words. However, I persisted and got to the end. Reading such books opened up many secrets for me. My interest in Urdu and Persian literature developed into a passion, and I embarked upon the Persian odes of Anvari and Khaqani.* However I soon grew tired of their false flattery, and locked them away in my book-case. These days I read newspapers and learn a lot about what is going on in the world.

Because I have been careful with my money, I have enough saved up to keep me going for the rest of my life. I have repented of my sins with a true heart, and do my best to say my prayers regularly. It is true that I still live like a whore, and whether I live or die, I could not let myself be suffocated by observing purdah. However, I pray for those women who veil themselves, and wish them every blessing in their happily married lives.

I have some parting advice to those who follow my profession, and urge them to take heed of it.

'My poor, simple prostitutes! Never entertain the false hope that any man will ever love you with a true heart. The lover who gives his body and soul to you will depart in a few days. He will never settle down with you, and you are not even worthy of that. Only the virtuous, who see one face and never turn to another, will have the pleasure of true love. You, women of the street, will never find such a blessing from God. What was to happen to me happened. I am resigned to this and have fulfilled all my wishes. I have no desires left, though desire is a curse that never leaves you till your dying day. I hope that you will profit from this account of my life. I end it with a verse and hope for your prayer:

My dying day draws near. Perhaps, oh Life,
My very soul has had its fill of thee.'

Notes to Text

page

xv.	*Chowk*	:	the name of one the largest bazaars in Lucknow, where the courtesans lived.
xviii.	*metre and rhyme*	:	invitations to a *mushaira* would often carry a verse in the metre and rhyme-scheme of which participants would be asked to compose their own poem.
xx.	*language of women*	:	humorous poems were sometimes composed in the language and Idiom of women, known in Urdu as *rekhti.*

xvii. *Rusva; Ada* : the pen-names of the author and Umrao Jan respectively. For the use of pen-names, see Introduction.

xxix. *Mir, Mirza* : the names of two of the most famous Lucknow poets, Mir Babar Ali Anis and Mirza Dabir, who were renowned for their elegies on the Battle of Karbala. The reference could also be to the two celebrated 18th century Delhi poets, Mir Taqi Mir and Mirza Muhammad Rafi Sauda, both of whom spent their last days in Lucknow.

xxxii. *Qais* : the Arab noble, also known as Majnun 'the madman,' who lost his reason when he fell in love with Laila. The love-story of Laila and Majnun is the subject of many Persian and Urdu romances.

xxxiv. *blackness in your teeth and eyes* : women used to apply black powder, known as *missi,* to their teeth, and collyrium, known as *kajal,* to their eyes.

xxxv. *ustad* : a teacher or mentor, especially of students of music and poetry. The *ustad* was always paid great respect by pupils.

2. *Bahu Begum* : the wife of the second ruler of Avadh, whose tomb is situated in Faizabad.

Jamedar : the holder of a humble official post, such as door-keeper.

17. *pan* : betel-leaf, usually filled with areca nuts, lime, catechu and other ingredients, which is folded into a triangular shape and offered to guests.

19. *Bangla* : the old name for Faizabad, where the first buildings were temporary constructions known as *bangla* (from which the English word 'bungalow' is derived).

19. *Umrao Jan* : a courtesan added the suffix *Jan* to her name after she had been introduced to her first client.

25. *maulvi* : an educated man, who knows Arabic and who is capable of imparting religious instruction.

26. *Soil of Karbala* : the maulvi would have been a Shi'a, and his rosary would have come from Karbala, the area in Iraq where Husain was martyred. A Sunni maulvi's rosary would have come from Mecca.

The education described here is the traditional syllabus of Arabic and Persian texts, which are still

		widely prescribed in Muslim schools.
29.	*domni*	: a female singer; a member of the Dom caste. Cf. 'Romany' gypsy.
36.	*missi*	: black powder applied to the teeth (see note to p. xxxi) as a sign of beauty. Here the term is used to denote a prostitute's deflowering.
39.	*bawdy songs*	: at weddings women traditionally sing bawdy songs, which would of course be unacceptable on any other occasion. The tradition is known as *gali gana.*
48.	*Atish, Nasikh*	: the names of two famous 19th century Urdu poets of Lucknow.
55.	*ashrafis*	: the name of a gold coin, used in Lucknow during the Royal Period.
58.	*Ayaz*	: the name of the slave of the Afghan emperor, Mahmud Ghaznavi. Ayaz's servitude is proverbial.
68.	*soz*	: verses mourning the death of Husain which were set to music. The art, which has now declined, was highly prized.
69.	*majlis*	: gatherings organized mainly by Shi'as during the month of Muharram to commemorate the death of Husain. Such ceremonies were usually prolonged for forty days.

69. *elegy* : a long Urdu verse composition, known as *marsiya,* on some aspect of the Battle of Karbala.

87. *Laila's dog* : Laila loves Majnun (see note to p. xxx)

91. *Baiswara* : a province in Awadh, named after the Bais tribe of Rajputs.

94. *bride of the fourth day* : on the fourth day after the marriage, the bride and bridegroom visit the bride's parents. For the ceremony, known as *chauti,* the bride is always beautifully dressed.

124. *elegies* : see note to page 69.

Anis, Dabir : see note on page xxix.

125. *Hyderabad, Deccan* : Hyderabad in the south of India was the capital of the Nizam's state. After the fall of Avadh in 1857, many Muslim families moved there.

128. *tying the knot* : i.e. 'to mark the year.' The Persian word for 'birthday,' *salgira,* literally means 'year-knot.'

139. *dirge* : the song known as *soz.* See note to page 57.

140. *fast* : a reference to the *hazari roza* or 'thousand-fold fast,' which

			is celebrated on the 27th of Rajab as the anniversary of the Prophet's ascent to heaven. The Queen and Birjis Qadr left Lucknow for Nepal on the 16th of March, 1858 (29 Rajab 1274 A.H.).
145.	*Bahu Begum*	:	see note to page 2.
153.	*Qais, Laila*	:	see note to page xxxii
160.	*leech*	:	imbibing a leech is said to cause infertility in women.
169.	*new moon*	:	the day of the new moon, which marks the beginning of the Muslim month, is regarded as a good day for visiting shrines.
	Hazrat Abbas	:	the younger brother of Husain, who was also killed at Karbala. Umrao Jan, since she does not observe purdah, can freely enter the men's enclosure of the shrine.
	Traditions of the Prophet	:	the Arabic texts, known as *Hadith,* which are regarded second in importance to the Quran.
174.	*replica of Husain's tomb*	:	i.e. the *taziya,* which on the 10th of Muharram was paraded through the streets.

194.	*Khalil Khan*	:	'when Khalil Khan flew his doves' is a proverbial expression for 'the glorious past.'
199.	*Gulistan*	:	one of the great Persian classics written by Saadi in the 13th century.
	Akhlaq-e-Nasiri	:	a 13th century Persian work on ethics, noted for its complicated style.
	Anvari, Khaqani	:	two 12th century Persian poets who are especially noted for their eulogies *(qasida)*.